T0266829

Beyond Return on Investment

Expanding the Value of Healthcare
Information Technology

Second Edition

Beyond Return on Investment

Expanding the Value of Healthcare Information Technology

Second Edition

Pam W. Arlotto
Susan P. Irby

CRC Press
Taylor & Francis Group
Boca Raton   London   New York

CRC Press is an imprint of the
Taylor & Francis Group, an **informa** business
A PRODUCTIVITY PRESS BOOK

CRC Press
Taylor & Francis Group
6000 Broken Sound Parkway NW, Suite 300
Boca Raton, FL 33487-2742

© 2019 by Taylor & Francis Group, LLC
CRC Press is an imprint of Taylor & Francis Group, an Informa business

No claim to original U.S. Government works

Printed on acid-free paper

International Standard Book Number-13: 978-1-138-36732-6 (Paperback)
978-1-138-36810-1 (Hardback)

Visit the Taylor & Francis Web site at
http://www.taylorandfrancis.com

and the CRC Press Web site at
http://www.crcpress.com

Contents

List of Figures

List of Tables

Foreword

"The return on investment of information technology" is a dangerous phrase. The phrase can mislead the investing organization to believe that

- Financial returns are the most appropriate (or only) measure of the worth of the investment.
- The returns can be achieved by a passive (or moderately active) investor. Invest funds, monitor progress, and await the returns.
- The cost of the investment is the only direct cost of consequence.
- At some point, the fruits of the investment are harvested, and the process of obtaining a return is over. The house is sold or the child finishes college.
- The investor is largely unchanged by the investment. While enjoying his or her retirement, the investor is no smarter, taller, or wittier than when he or she was working.

Investments in healthcare information technology (HIT) are not (or should not be) considered in this way.

The returns of an investment in HIT are complex and multifaceted. Improvements in service, enhancements to decision making, regulatory compliance, and, at times, true organizational transformation join financial returns as measures of worth.

Achieving true value from the HIT investment often requires extensive redesign of processes, innovating new ways to do work, significant change in organization structure and staff behavior, and recasting of the organization's view of itself. This is very difficult and challenging work—there is nothing passive about it.

The costs of HIT, although not insignificant, pale when compared to the costs of changing the organization. Staff time spent changing processes, learning new ways of doing work, and coping with what are often rocky transitions may not result in a measurable expense, but the costs are real.

Although the organization may have near-term goals for its HIT investment, the challenge of leveraging HIT to improve operational performance and elevate the quality and safety of care never ends. There will never be a time when any organization will be able to say, "We are done. We cannot perform any better than we do today."

When truly successful in its HIT investments, the organization will be materially different. The organization may still deliver patient care or conduct biomedical research, but its processes will be significantly more efficient and effective, and its performance should be noticeably superior.

The value that HIT can enable is significant. Moreover, obtaining this value may be necessary if the healthcare organization is to thrive in an era of value-based care and population health. However, obtaining the value is a substantial management and clinical challenge.

Pam W. Arlotto and Susan P. Irby have done a superb job of describing how healthcare organizations can address these challenges. *Beyond Return on Investment: Expanding the Value of Healthcare Information Technology, Second Edition* clearly outlines and discusses critical areas, such as the organization's technology adoption culture, governance, the partnership between the information technology leadership and the rest of the organization, value management, the management of change, and the measurement and monitoring of value realization efforts.

Obtaining HIT value is a leadership undertaking that is vastly more complex and difficult than selecting and installing the right application from the right vendor with the right return on investment financial projection.

Healthcare organizations will be well served by this book.

John Glaser, PhD
Senior Vice President
Cerner Corporation

Preface

> The greatest danger in times of turbulence is not the turbulence – it is to act with yesterday's logic.

> **—Peter Drucker**

In 2002, a casual conversation at a HIMSS conference led to the creation of a basic primer on the return on investment (ROI) of healthcare information technology (HIT). At the time, HIMSS members within hospitals and at solution vendors were challenged to move beyond basic cost–benefit analysis. They needed justification of IT expenditures as part of the hospital annual budget process. The primary message in the primer was implementation of HIT alone does not result in ROI. A greater value story is needed, and values must be managed into reality.

Seventeen years and four books later, the healthcare industry is much more complex and most hospitals and providers have adopted electronic health records and applications, such as enterprise resource management, revenue management, and business intelligence. Innovative cloud-based solutions are reinventing the way our clinicians work and disrupting our business models. While many things have changed, values still must be managed into reality. Implementation alone will not suffice.

The following chapters modernize the concept of ROI and extend the concept of value beyond realization to value creation and transformation. We wrote this book for the clinical, business, and HIT leaders alike. It provides frameworks, examples, and practical steps for managing values into reality. For more information regarding these concepts or to contact the authors, you may reach us at info@maestrostrategies.com or view our website at www.maestrostrategies.com.

Pam W. Arlotto
Atlanta, Georgia, December 2018

Acknowledgments

This book is dedicated to our healthcare clients and colleagues. We thank you for your vision of a healthcare system transformed through the power of data, technology, and innovative change. Your hard work is inspirational. Appreciation is extended to Sherry Gettmann and Jamie Lovett for their diligence during the editing process. We are grateful to our family and friends who have supported us during our careers and the countless hours we have given to making this series of books possible.

About the Authors

Pam W. Arlotto, MBA, FHIMSS, is CEO and President of Maestro Strategies, LLC, a management consulting firm focused on transformation and the orchestration of change in the healthcare industry. Ms. Arlotto created the award-winning series *Return on Investment: Maximizing the Value of Healthcare Information Technology* and has co-authored three previous books on planning for and realizing the value of information technology (IT). This groundbreaking book provides an overall management system for governing, planning for, realizing, and creating value and return on investment. She has held a number of important healthcare and industry leadership positions that include

- Board of Trustees member, Georgia Tech Foundation
- Advisory Board member, Wallace H. Coulter School of Biomedical Engineering at Georgia Tech and Emory University, Scheller College of Business at Georgia Tech
- National President and Fellow, Healthcare Information and Management Systems Society (HIMSS)
- Adjunct faculty member, Healthcare Informatics program at University of Alabama at Birmingham
- Board member, numerous privately held companies and not-for-profit organizations

Ms. Arlotto is a popular and frequent speaker at healthcare industry and corporate meetings and has authored a number of journal and magazine articles.

Susan P. Irby, MSHS, is the Managing Director of Business Intelligence and Analytics for Maestro Strategies, LLC, and has over 30 years of healthcare experience with providers and as a consultant. Ms. Irby built the firm's ROI Toolkit and specializes in financial planning, decision support, and IT benefits realization. Her experience includes

- Transformation strategy advisory consulting work, including planning for care management platforms, enterprise analytics management systems, clinical integration, and population health management for a variety of health systems
- Return on investment and value management strategies for health systems, solution companies, and associations
- Director of Strategic Planning and Decision Support, Alta Bates Health System, where she pioneered early decision support system and benefits realizations applications in healthcare
- Arthur Young consultant with experience in strategic planning, operating and capital budgeting, cost accounting, financial planning, and forecasting

Chapter 1

Introduction: Setting the Stage for Value Creation

Purpose

To introduce value creation while revisiting and expanding the healthcare information technology (HIT) concepts of return on investment (ROI) and value realization.

In this chapter, the reader will review

- The evolving definition of return on investment and value as it relates to healthcare information technology
- The journey from Meaningful Use to High-Value Healthcare
- Incremental performance improvement to transformation and innovative disruption, the growing scope of healthcare change
- Expansion of key value themes

Background

In 2003, in the award-winning book *Return on Investment: Maximizing the Value of Healthcare Information Technology,* the first in a series of three books, return on investment (ROI) was described as an essential step in comparing, selecting, prioritizing, and measuring healthcare information technology (HIT) strategies and investments. The authors proposed that ROI was not enough to drive investments in HIT. Value, or impact on enterprise performance, must be demonstrated and managed into reality. Traditional information technology (IT) justification models focused on the technology and its requirements and cost, all but ignoring the business plans and strategic direction of the organization. Expensive to acquire, implement, and maintain, HIT, in and of itself, would not justify the capital and operating outlay required to justify the commitment of funds. The first book served as a primer for conducting an ROI and value analysis for a single IT project or software program. In 2007, the second book in the series, *Beyond Return on Investment: Expanding the Value of Healthcare Information Technology*, provided a framework for the enterprise to manage the value of a portfolio of HIT projects and programs. Given the significant change in the healthcare industry and in HIT, we released this book, the second edition of *Beyond Return on Investment: Expanding the Value of Healthcare Information Technology* in 2019.

With value as the goal, HIT's ability to enable performance improvement through improved business and clinical outcomes, reduced cost, and enhanced patient experience was examined in both quantitative and qualitative terms. In fact, rather than just focusing on traditional measures of ROI, the value of HIT was defined as the degree of change in the business and clinical outcomes as compared to the total IT and business investment.

$$\text{Value of HIT} = \frac{\text{Degree of Change Business and Clinical Outcomes}}{\text{Total IT and Business Investment}}$$

In the intervening years, the Health Information Technology for Economic and Clinical Health (HITECH) Act of 2009 introduced the concept of the meaningful use (MU) of electronic health record (EHR) systems. Over $38 billion in financial incentives have been paid to more than 5000 hospitals and 500,000 physicians. No other sector of the US economy of comparable size and complexity has undergone such rapid computerization.[1] In order to receive payment from the MU program, providers and hospitals had to demonstrate the use of certified EHR technology:

- In a meaningful manner (e.g., electronic prescribing)
- For the electronic exchange of health information to improve quality of healthcare
- To submit clinical quality measures

The concept of MU rested on five pillars of health-outcomes policy priorities, including goals to

- Improve quality, safety, efficiency, and reducing health disparities
- Engage patients and families in their health
- Improve care coordination
- Improve population and public health
- Ensure adequate privacy and security protection for personal health information[2]

The third book in the series, *Rethinking Return on Investment: The Challenge of Accountable Meaningful Use*, challenged healthcare leaders to examine their strategic view of HIT return on investment and value. Rather than IT business cases that focused on project- or initiative-based savings, such as streamlined staffing, reduced supply cost, or error elimination, a more strategic view that encompassed redesign of care delivery and reimbursement models with

Not worried, believe their vendor has them covered, focused on compliance & minimal reporting

Focused EHR functionality. Haven't separated IT implementation from MU preparation

Understand connection between MU and future reimbursement & care delivery models. Have plans to develop care coordination & clinical decision support

Have created an Integrated Road Map that includes clinical workflow & change management with EHR implementation

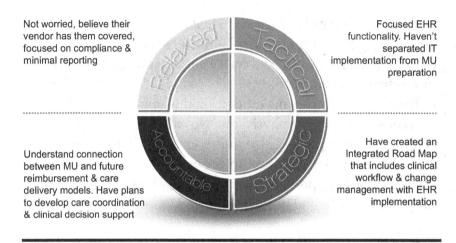

Figure 1.1   Strategic approaches to meaningful use.

a larger impact on the Triple Aim was necessary. The book introduced the concept of *accountable meaningful use* and identified four categories healthcare organizations could select as their approach to MU, as shown in Figure 1.1.

The categories include

■ *Relaxed*: These organizations were not worried. They had confidence in their HIT vendor to a fault. They felt they were implementing *certified electronic health record* technology, and they planned to do just enough to receive the incentive payments. These health systems bought into a common misperception—that implementing EHR technology alone automatically demonstrated MU and value.

■ *Tactical*: Many organizations approached MU as a tactical endeavor. They had a clinical system application plan but did not develop an organizational change management plan for MU. While they recognized the mutual responsibilities of the vendor and provider, they only viewed MU from the perspective of technology implementation.

■ *Strategic*: Health systems at this level viewed information technology as a strategic asset. They understood that successful MU of EHRs was not an IT project but an organizational change project. These health systems created an integrated road map that included workflow redesign before the implementation of systems. Wary of automating broken processes, they spent time planning and invested in clinical informatics, process redesign, and project management.

■ *Accountable*: For these rare organizations, the future of healthcare was/is focused on using information in new and different ways to redesign care delivery and reimbursement models across venues of care. Even though only a few organizations planned for the accountable MU of EHRs, they continue to serve as the industry standard. Forward looking, they designed evidence-based systems of care, provided clinical decision support at the point of care, and turned data into knowledge by reporting key quality measures, changing the way they deliver care to better manage populations and positively influence outcomes.

In surveys of MU readiness, most US hospitals approached MU in a relaxed or tactical view. Less than 10% were truly accountable. For the most part, EHRs were implemented to support one entity and automate existing processes within that organization—a hospital, a clinic, or a practice. To meet MU requirements and receive incentive payments, organizations took a check-the-box approach from a regulatory standpoint and a big-bang approach from an enterprise-implementation perspective. Most planned to *optimize* their EHRs at a later point in time. Today, definitions of *optimization* vary widely across the industry: for some it consists of routine maintenance, for others it involves remediation of technical issues not addressed during implementation, for others it includes the addition of new functionality, and for the performance-improvement minded, it includes standardization of processes and application of best practices. At best, these approaches produce incremental performance improvement and change, resulting in a nominal return on investment and value.

Even though the federal government's HITECH investment was momentous, it was only a beginning. In 2017, estimates of the continued HIT investment vary widely from $31 billion to $148 billion annually,[3] including

- Federal projects such as the Department of Veterans Affairs' and Department of Defense's efforts to modernize their EHRs.
- Hospitals, physician practices, and large health systems are seeking to leverage their EHR data through analytics and care-management systems.
- The Centers for Medicare & Medicaid Services (CMS) and private payers are experimenting with alternative reimbursement models that emphasize quality and require IT infrastructure for success.
- Consumers are exploring telehealth and mobile health along with wearables and home diagnostic tools.
- Digital health deals by investors are at an all-time high in terms of the number of deals and dollars raised, with 2018 mid-year investments of $3.4 billion projected to outpace those of 2017.[4]

Notwithstanding the progress in adoption and continued expenditures, many providers and health-system leaders have complained about the increased documentation burden, the usability of the systems, the ongoing interoperability gaps, the maintenance costs, etc. A recent Harris poll conducted on behalf of Stanford Medicine indicates that even though roughly two-thirds of primary care physicians think EHRs have led to improved care and are somewhat satisfied with their EHRs, they continue to report problems. The majority believe that EHRs contribute to physician burn-out and need a complete overhaul, 71% and 59%, respectively.[5]

Given the sea change that is occurring on multiple fronts across the healthcare industry—consolidation, consumerism, provider-payer convergence, etc.—incremental change is no longer enough. As the industry shifts away from fee-for-service medicine, 76% of healthcare leaders report positive ROI from their early experiments in value-based care. At the same time, 64% of these leaders say EHRs don't do enough to support the new care and reimbursement models. In a *Harvard Business Review* article entitled, "We Interviewed Healthcare Leaders about Their Industry and They're Worried," Poku and Schulman report, "the technology needs of the emerging population-health strategy differ significantly from those of the current fee-for-service model...there is a growing realization that the transformation of the health care system will require existing organizations to develop new business models and new organizational structures."[6]

In hindsight, IT ROI and value realization have been elusive when implemented in a fragmented, antiquated healthcare-delivery system. The transition to high-value healthcare will accelerate the requirement to connect organizations, people, processes, data, and devices in new and different ways. Value will be created as markets, the workforce, networks, and customer relationships are redefined. Results, in the form of reduced complexity, improved outcomes, new service models, increased cost savings, and more, will be possible.

The Healthcare IT Value Pathway

There exists a full spectrum of potential value that can be realized from investment in HIT and digital tools with the objective of changing healthcare business and clinical performance. The Healthcare Value Pathway, in Figure 1.2, shows that value can be realized at multiple levels: from automation, from process improvement, from strategic care delivery redesign through disruptive innovation, and the

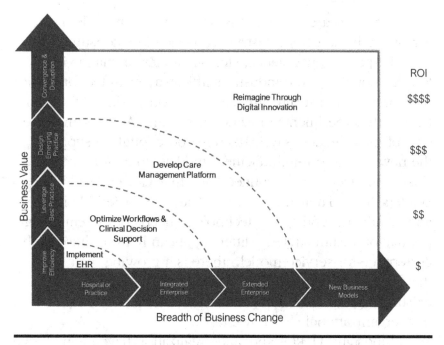

Figure 1.2   The healthcare value pathway.

pathway demonstrates that as one moves from automation to innovation, the potential benefits expand.

Value and the ultimate return on investment will occur as the healthcare industry is transformed from volume to value, through clinically integrated, consumer (patient) centric, connected health and care. While fee-for-service reimbursement is still the predominant form of payment in many markets, value-based care and population health are no longer experiments. Accountable care organizations (ACOs) and clinically integrated networks (CINs) are critical components of today's healthcare ecosystem and must scale as organizations take on more covered lives. In the past, brick-and-mortar facilities served as the centerpiece of the healthcare enterprise; today and tomorrow, digital care management platforms will connect care teams and patients. Technology is pervasive, touching all aspects of health and healthcare delivery. New information-based modalities and precision medicine provide the ability to prevent disease and prolong life expectancy through more comprehensive management of chronic illness. Healthcare organizations will need to develop comprehensive transformation strategies, design new business models, and orchestrate new ways of working, decision-making, and organizing, while simultaneously divesting a broad array of legacy assets and cultures.

Value Themes

The healthcare industry has spent billions of dollars on EHRs and other advanced systems. Adoption has soared, but the return on investment and value is still questioned. In this the second edition of *Beyond Return on Investment: Expanding the Value of Healthcare Information Technology*, the concepts and lessons learned are modernized from years of researching, consulting, speaking, and writing on this topic. Much has changed since the 2003 publication of the first book in the series; yet, much remains the same. Early conversations identified several Value Themes that bear repeating/expanding and include:

- *Technology is a means to an end, not the ultimate goal*: Many healthcare leaders continue to see HIT as a silver bullet rather than as part of a total solution that starts with strategy; new operating models; redesigned processes, behaviors and structures; and change management.
- *Value must be planned for, managed, measured—and accountability assigned*: Many organizations estimate ROI or predict value as part of an IT selection process or in conjunction with the development of the annual budget. Now, however, a formal Value-Management program that spans the entire life of the investment is necessary. Rather than just implementing and optimizing systems, healthcare

leaders need a robust plan for value in the form of outcomes improvement and cost reduction, new consumer relationships and activated patients, agile and effective care processes, etc.

■ *Change can be disruptive, transformative, incremental, or targeted*: Each organization should define its readiness for change, specific strategic goals for change, and the investment required to make this level of change happen. Historically, healthcare has been a change-averse industry, with the bulk of mainstream organizations lagging other industries. Yet, innovators today are reinventing the industry at an unprecedented speed and scale.

■ *New governance structures and leadership capabilities are needed to drive change*: Just as medical staff committees, traditional quality departments, and siloed-based institutional management structures were not designed to lead the transition to high-value healthcare, the IT function within most healthcare systems is not prepared to design new approaches to care or the business of healthcare. As care management and reimbursement models change, new clinically integrated decision-making and oversight structures will be needed to govern, prioritize, and ensure accountability for change. New capabilities in design thinking, informatics, analytics, and innovation will be needed.

■ *Enterprise value realization is no longer the goal— value creation for the extended community is essential*: Historically, most healthcare systems focused on enterprise ROI and value realization. In the future, new value will be created across community, region, state, nation, and beyond through digital capabilities that provide new ways to collaborate, connect, and leverage data to make smarter decisions and to simplify the way we work and create outcome-driven customer experiences.

For those interested in a more in-depth exploration of the implications of high-value healthcare and population health, please refer to *Rethinking Return on Investment: The Challenge of Population Health Management.* This next book in the series focuses on changing the way the healthcare industry changes. Value Maps help facilitate conversation and work to ensure return on investment and value creation for the post-meaningful use era.

Conclusion

Healthcare has always been known as a change-averse industry. Despite this perceived tendency, the industry has in fact undergone significant change since we explored the original topic of ROI for HIT in our first book in 2003. Revisiting this topic now prepares us to look to the future with anticipation at the dramatic changes on the horizon. The healthcare industry has only begun to realize the value of IT and now has the opportunity to create new value.

Endnotes

1. Halamka, J. D. and M. Tripathi. "The HITECH Era in Retrospect." *New England Journal of Medicine.* September 7, 2017. https://www.nejm.org/doi/full/10.1056/NEJMp1709851.
2. "Medicare & Medicaid EHR Incentive Program Meaningful Use Stage 1 Requirements Overview." CMS.gov Centers for Medicare & Medicaid Services. 2011. https://www.cms.gov/Regulations-and-Guidance/Legislation/EHRIncentivePrograms/.
3. "How Much Will the U.S. Health IT Market Be worth in 2017?" Cognitive Medical Systems. August 23, 2016. http://cognitivemedicalsystems.com/much-will-u-s-health-market-worth-2017/.
4. Zweig, M., H. Tecco, and M. Wang. "2018 Midyear Funding Review: Digital Health Déjà Vu in Yet Another Record Breaking Half." Rock Health. 2018. https://rockhealth.com/reports/2018-midyear-funding-review-digital-

health-deja-vu-in-yet-another-record-breaking-half/?mc_
cid=9003ae7ad9.

5. Standford Medicine. *How Doctors Feel About Electronic Health Records National Physician Poll by The Harris Poll.* Report. 2018.

6. Schulman, M. P. and A. Kevin. "We Interviewed Health Care Leaders About Their Industry, and They're Worried." *Harvard Business Review.* April 5, 2017. hbr.org/2016/12/we-interviewed-health-care-leaders-about-their-industry-and-theyre-worried.

Chapter 2

The Journey to High-Value Healthcare: Understanding the Leadership Pivot

Purpose

To explore the transition from volume to value and present a framework for the three stages of change each health system will experience during the move from fee-for-service to value-based care and the evolving role of leadership at each stage.

In this chapter, the reader will learn

- The differences in brick-and-mortar, transitional, and digital health, connected health stages in the transition to value-based care
- The integrated roles of IT, Informatics, Analytics, and Quality in the virtuous cycle of value management

- The five layers of the Care Management Platform and its role in preparing for population health and the assumption of risks
- Leadership models for each stage of the transition

The Journey to High-Value Healthcare

The healthcare industry has begun the shift to high-value healthcare through a variety of new incentive programs focused on reimbursing providers based on the quality rather than the quantity of care they give to their patients. With the Centers for Medicare & Medicaid Services (CMS) initially leading the way, new payment programs such as Hospital Acquired Conditions Reduction, Value-Based Purchasing, and Readmission Reduction; the Merit-Based Incentive Payment System; Alternative Payment Programs including Medicare Shared Savings, ACO Track 1+, Next Generation ACO, Bundle Payments, etc.; and a variety of other initiatives encourage providers to deliver high-quality care and to spend healthcare dollars more wisely. Simultaneously, commercial payers are escalating their rollout of value-based programs. According to a June 2018 study by Change Healthcare, 120 participating payers report that today "nearly two-thirds of payments are based on value."[1]

While the pursuit of high-value healthcare is a common theme for health systems, physician groups, and payers alike, the degree of change is unique for each market, health system, payer, and individual provider. There is no "one-size-fits-all" formula or model. With variations on the timing, pace of change, and numbers/types of payment agreements, many prioritize clinical integration, quality measurement and improvement, and development of a care management infrastructure. Most start as targeted experiments and scale as the number of covered lives expand, care management

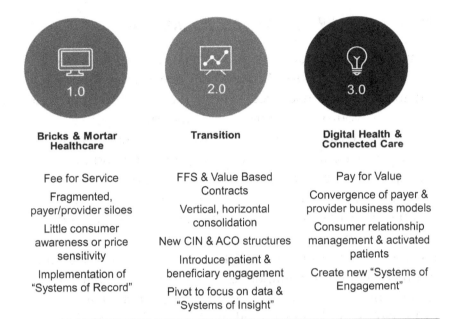

Figure 2.1   The journey to high-value healthcare.

models are designed, and new capabilities are developed. The framework in Figure 2.1 may help clarify the shift.

The transition starts with technology enabling the fragmented delivery system and its components. As new capabilities and competencies are developed, technology integrates the extended enterprise across the care continuum, partners, and affiliates of the enterprise. Ultimately, the health and healthcare delivery platforms of the future will create new value through customer-centric digital innovations. Massive change will occur not only in the technology but also in the value chains, organization structures, leadership roles, clinical and business processes, and revenue models. For established health systems, sweeping redesign of legacy assets alongside strategic initiatives that include consolidation, regulatory compliance, growth, transformation, and innovation will be necessary. Understanding both the business and technology implications of each stage of the journey is essential.

Stage 1.0: Brick-and-Mortar Healthcare

Healthcare's outmoded fee-for-service (FFS) payment model has its origins in a pre–World War II economy as traditional indemnity health insurance—you get a service, submit your claim, and your insurer covers your incurred expenses. Employers began offering these insurance benefits as a way to attract employees.[2] Post-war prosperity and low unemployment expanded these benefits, and in 1965, as part of President Lyndon B. Johnson's "War on Poverty" and the "Great Society," Congress enacted Medicaid and Medicare to provide similar access to and payment for care for the indigent and elderly. Yet, today many Americans are not receiving the recommended care, and nearly half of all Americans suffer from chronic diseases such as diabetes or hypertension.[3] In fact, total health spending is expected to rise to 20% or one-fifth of the GDP by 2025, and today, 57 and 76 million are enrolled in Medicare and Medicaid, respectively. The Institute of Medicine estimates that 30% of spending, or $765 billion, goes to unnecessary, ineffective, overpriced, and wasteful services.[4]

This fragmented healthcare delivery system has allowed hospitals and physicians to practice medicine their own way, which encouraged customization of EHR systems according to individual physician and hospital needs and generated little market demand for enterprise or population-level features such as common technical standards, decision support for adherence to guidelines, measurement capability for population health, or interoperability for coordination across care settings.[5] Yet, Stage 1.0's *systems of record* serve multiple important purposes. These transaction systems, designed to collect and store data, have the ability to generate routine operational reports. The systems are foundational to future efforts to improve outcomes, reduce cost, and enhance the patient experience. Weaknesses of EHRs during this stage include limited interoperability and the proprietary nature of the systems, implementations that do not consider workflow, usability, clinician productivity, etc., and the lack of connection with the patient.

Stage 2.0: Transition

The transition stage, or Stage 2.0, brings the inevitable migration beyond the enterprise EHR. New capabilities are required to coordinate care and manage the health of populations across the continuum and with affiliates and partners. The focus must move from adoption to creation of *systems of insight* and support of new value-based contracts, clinical integration networks, and accountable care organizations. While most organizations have not reached the "tipping point" where approximately two-thirds of their covered lives are at risk, expanded competencies in informatics, analytics, and quality must complement existing IT skills (Figure 2.2).

New highly configurable and open Care Management Platforms will meet the evolving needs of the new marketplace (Figure 2.3). Requirements will include:

■ Patient and consumer-centric data exchange that follows the patient across providers, networks, geographies, and payer relationships

"There is a virtuous cycle created by having the foundational IT systems in place, applying health informatics skills to help make the systems 'smart', building analytics capabilities to inform decision making and partnering with quality to drive performance improvement and transformed care processes."

John Fox, President & CEO, Beaumont Health
Source: Maestro UniversityHealth Consortium Research, 2015

Figure 2.2   The virtuous cycle of value management: informatics, quality, analytics, and IT.

CONSUMER & PATIENT ENGAGEMENT

24/7 Access via Unified Portal, Self Service Scheduling, Branded Call Centers, Customer Relationship Management, Patient Self Reported Data, Linguistic Services, Remote Monitoring, Patient Education, Telehealth/mHealth & Telemedicine, etc.

ADVANCED CARE MANAGEMENT

Health Risk Assessment, Care Management, Case Management, Care Planning, Adherence Alerts, Disease Management, Risk Management, Referral Management, Rules Based Workflows, etc.

KNOWLEDGE MANAGEMENT & ANALYTICS

Data Governance, Business Intelligence, Care Protocols, Claims Data, Point of Care Clinical Decision Support, Metrics, Data Mining, Predictive Modeling, etc.

HEALTH INFORMATION EXCHANGE

Master Patient Index, Secure Messaging, Standards based Interoperability, Communication Tools, Referral Tracking, Community Health Record, Registries, etc.

FOUNDATIONAL SYSTEMS

Payers · Rx · Diagnostics · Post Acute Providers · Hospitals · Specialists · PCMH

Figure 2.3   The care-management platform.

- Analytics capabilities that integrate demographic, financial, clinical, claims, and other sources of data to risk stratify and manage attributed patients
- Workflow-driven care coordination and management capabilities to support care teams, including primary care and specialty physicians; care management nurses, therapists, social workers, nutritionists, and educators; patients and their families; and others from a variety of community agencies and support networks
- New tools for consumer health and patient engagement in planning and improving their health

For a more in-depth discussion of The Care Management Platform and the requirements for population health, see the book *Rethinking Return on Investment: The Challenge of Population Health Management.* From an HIT perspective, a cultural *pivot* is necessary to move from 1.0, which focused on EHR adoption, to 2.0, which emphasizes value management. Rather than the traditional *implementation thinking* associated with EHR deployment, Value Management must become the focus. Differences are described in Table 2.1.

Stage 2.0 provides each organization the opportunity to learn and experiment with new models before scaling and assuming the risk for high numbers of attributed patients.

Stage 3.0: Digital Health and Connected Care

While changes in the reimbursement systems will continue to influence the move from the 1.0 *sick-care* system to 2.0, *prevention and management of chronic conditions,* by 3.0 a new force will be at play. According to a July 2018 McKinsey healthcare consumer research report, "Consumers want more from the healthcare industry including the best coverage, increased customer service, lower cost, and improved access. A growing number of consumers think that healthcare organizations should offer them digital tools at par with those

Table 2.1   Implementation v. Value Management Thinking

Implementation Thinking	Value Management Thinking
Treats technology in isolation	Integrates people, process, information, technology, and change
Focuses on the micro-view of the patient-physician relationship, and the episodic nature of care delivery	Focuses on the macro-view of the comprehensive care needed by a population, including wellness and prevention; chronic condition management; acute, post-acute, and palliative care
Supports one entity or provider	Supports the continuum of care and the entire care team, including the patient
Automates existing business models	Transforms business models
Led by IT	Led by the business
Focuses on application functionality	Focuses on data and customer engagement
Focuses on projects	Focuses on strategic programs
Increases costs	Increases results

offered by companies in other industries."[6] Leaders of the disruption will come from entrepreneurs as well as payer-provider partnerships in which health systems take on health-plan functions to become *payviders*. Payers expand traditional disease and care management responsibilities to bring new personalized products to their customers, employers expand their influence, and players from adjacent market spaces use digital technology to drive increased levels of change. Along with an explosion of data, technologies such as artificial intelligence, machine learning, social, mobile, the internet-of-things, genomics, etc. will accelerate the pace and degree of change. Forward-thinking healthcare leaders will increasingly design *systems of behavior* to create new digital value chains that transform their organizations and their services to their customers.

The Leadership Pivot

The phrase "a foot in two canoes" has been used in recent years to describe the fact that "many hospitals and health systems are rowing upstream – with a bit of choppy water. The smaller canoe is value-based care, and many are trying to find stable footing. The other shoe remains firmly planted in the larger fee-for-service or volume canoe."[7] Given the uncertainty that often accompanies such change, many healthcare leaders resist new payment models and place a sense of security in the status quo. Faced with this unpredictability and chaotic level of change, some healthcare leaders have chosen to avoid making decisions and wait for the situation to return to normal, while others look for a silver bullet—a path, product, or process that promises a simple, somewhat magical solution for the transition. Gary Kaplan, MD, Chairman and CEO of Virginia Mason Health System in Seattle, believes that for the foreseeable future, we will exist in a "hybrid model with varying payment schemes for differing populations." He states, "Payment for quality, even in its current nascent form, is already here, and no amount of resistance…is going to reverse this trend. Rather than straddling the two-payment model 'canoes,' it is time for physicians (and other healthcare leaders) to help sink fee-for-service and fully commit to aligning payment around value."[8]

To make progress along the journey, healthcare's traditional decision-making model will not work. Typically based on enterprise strategic-planning cycles that are completed every few years, aligned IT strategies are divided into plans that tie to annual budget processes. The ability to drive the transition from volume to value is too slow, too incremental, and too risk averse. Big-bang implementations no longer support the uncertain and ever-changing environment. Eric Ries, the creator of the *Lean Startup Methodology,* applies the term *pivot* to describe a shift in strategy—one that implies keeping one foot firmly on the ground as you shift the other in a new direction.[9] Leaders pivot by "making a structural course correction to test a new fundamental hypothesis about the product, strategy, and engine of growth."[10] Experimentation and targeted demonstration projects to explore new models prior to scaling is an important skill set for Stage 2.0 organizations.

Each stage in the journey to high-value healthcare will require unique leadership attributes, capabilities, processes, etc. The leadership pivot from command-and-control to collaborative organization and decision-making structures should begin prior to Stage 2.0. New leadership positions will evolve to drive targeted strategies and be responsible for value realization and creation. As Digital Health and Connected Care become a reality, return on investment through dramatic improvement in health, healthcare outcomes, total cost of care, and customer engagement will result. Table 2.2 examines the role of leadership at each stage, helping to depict the necessary pivot.

Conclusion

Each healthcare market, organization, and provider is at a different place on the journey to high-value healthcare. To move beyond incremental change, a leadership pivot should occur as organizations transition from Stage 1.0 to 2.0. Many struggle to balance fee-for-service and value-based reimbursement simultaneously. Chapter 3 will explore a targeted, agile approach to launching transformational activities and moving from tactical ROI to value realization and, ultimately, value creation.

Table 2.2 The Leadership Pivot

Stage	Brick-&-Mortar Healthcare 1.0	Transition 2.0	Digital Health & Connected Care 3.0
Enterprise Strategic Direction	• Fee-for-service reimbursement • Horizontal & vertical consolidation	• Clinical integration • Coordination of care • Quality measurement & reporting • Patient experience	• Risk management • Population health management • Consumerism • New business & care models
Leadership Domain	Acute care & physician practices	Continuum of care	Anytime, anywhere
Decision-Making Culture	Siloed—command & control, consensus	Dyads & matrixed—dotted lines, insight-driven decision-making	Collaboration, networked, predictive & prescriptive
Emerging Information & Technology Leadership	Chief Information Officer	Chief Medical Information Officer, Chief Quality Officer	Chief Health Information Officer, Chief Data Officer, Chief Transformation Officer, Chief Innovation Officer

(Continued)

Table 2.2 (Continued)   The Leadership Pivot

Stage	Brick-&-Mortar Healthcare 1.0	Transition 2.0	Digital Health & Connected Care 3.0
New Capabilities & Competencies	Meaningful use & EHR adoption	Interoperability, analytics, care management & patient engagement	Digital health, design thinking, innovation
ROI & Value Potential	Tactical benefits & ROI	Incremental value realization	Disruptive & transformational, value creation

Endnotes

1. "Finding the Value in Value-Based Care: The State of Value-Based Care in 2018." A Research Report Commissioned by Change Healthcare, 2018. https://Inspire.changehealthcare.com.
2. Barnes, J. "Moving Away from Fee-for-Service." *The Atlantic*. May 8, 2012. https://www.theatlantic.com/health/archive/2012/05/moving-away-from-fee-for-service/256755/.
3. Ibid.
4. "Infographic: U.S. Healthcare Spending." Peter G. Peterson Foundation. July 19, 2017. https://www.pgpf.org/infographic/infographic-us-healthcare-spending?utm_source=google.
5. Tripathi, M. "EHR Evolution: Policy and Legislation Forces Changing the HER." *Journal of AHIMA* 83, No. 10 (October 2012): 24–29.
6. Cordina, J., E. P. Jones, R. Kumar, and C. P. Martin. *Healthcare Consumerism 2018: An Update on the Journey.* McKinsey & Company, July 2018. https://www.mckinsey.com/industries/healthcare-systems-and-services/our-insights/healthcare-consumerism-2018.
7. Burrill, S. "2018 Outlook: Straddling Two Canoes." *Modern Healthcare*. Accessed July 16, 2018. http://www.modernhealthcare.com/article/20171213/SPONSORED/171219956.
8. Kaplan, G. S., and C. Craig Blackmore. "Time to Sink the Two Canoe Payment Models Argument.' *NEJM Catalyst* March 27, 2018. https://catalyst.nejm.org/sink-two-canoe-payment-models/.
9. Ries, E. *The Lean Startup: How Today's Entrepreneurs Use Continuous Innovation to Create Radically Successful Businesses.* New York: Crown Business, 2011.
10. Ibid.

Chapter 3

Chapter 3

Yesterday, Today, and Tomorrow: Transformation and Innovation

Purpose

To understand the definition of transformation and how this definition has changed over time.

In this chapter, the reader will learn to

- Consider the relationship between transformation and value
- Review the failures of the past
- Examine the implications of run, grow, and transform-on-demand rationalization
- Explore the future of digital transformation and innovation

Transformation: Yesterday v. Today

Transformation, a popular buzzword for over 20 years in healthcare and other industries, often refers to a change in management strategy with the aim of aligning the people, process, and technology initiatives of a company more closely with the organization's business strategy and vision.[1] The Office of the National Coordinator for Health Information Technology (ONC) recognized EHRs as the first step to transformed health care, with potential benefits, including

- Better health care by improving all aspects of patient care, including safety, effectiveness, patient-centeredness, communication, education, timeliness, efficiency, and equity
- Better health by encouraging healthier lifestyles in the entire population, including increased physical activity, better nutrition, avoidance of behavioral risks, and wider use of preventative care
- Improved efficiencies and lower healthcare costs by promoting preventative medicine and improved coordination of healthcare services, as well as by reducing waste and redundant tests
- Better clinical decision-making by integrating patient information from multiple sources[2]

Yet, the promised transformation has not occurred. In 2017, 61% of 1100 healthcare professionals surveyed indicated a poor or terrible return from their investment in EHRs as part of the HITECH and meaningful use incentives. An additional 29% reported mediocre results from this investment.[3] In fact, a growing body of evidence suggests unintended consequences resulting in HIT-induced medical error, harm, death, and other associated risks have increased significantly.[4] In his book *Guide to the Electronic Medical Record Practice: Strategies to Succeed, Pitfalls to Avoid*, Steven Arnold commented that "diving into technology without an understanding of how it relates to strategy and organization and behavioral changes is like diving into a swimming pool without filling it up first. It hurts if you land on your head."[5]

Michael Porter, in his landmark 2010 *New England Journal of Medicine* essay, "What is Value in Healthcare," espoused, "the current organizational structures and information systems of health care delivery make it challenging to measure (and deliver) value. Thus, most providers fail to do so."[6] In the past, we asked the wrong question: What is the return on investment of HIT? Instead, we should have asked: What results or outcomes are we seeking? Rather than aligning IT with the business or delivering IT return on investment to the business, today we understand there is no "IT value" separate from the business; they are one and the same. Increasingly, healthcare leaders understand that in the future, IT touches all we do. No longer just automating our work, IT is the way we work—how we segment our customer populations, how we deliver our clinical services, how we collaborate with our partners and affiliates, how we manage our supply chains, and how we manage our revenue streams and more.

Transformation of the healthcare industry is taking on new meaning. Once defined as "the most entrenched change averse industry in the United States,"[7] today's healthcare industry has no choice but to transform as it deals with simultaneous game-changing trends, such as

- Value-based care reimbursement programs from commercial and governmental payers
- Population-focused care management and delivery models
- Vertical and horizontal consolidation, as well as the convergence of providers and payers
- New-market entrants seeking to disrupt traditional business models
- Digitally aware consumers becoming more proactive in managing their health, and patients becoming more proactive in managing their own health outcomes

- New targeted therapeutics, smart diagnostics, advanced informatics, and digital technologies
- Increasing availability of genomic, health, and lifestyle data[8]

In a survey of 50 healthcare CEOs, "82% agreed that their organizations are being increasingly pressed to reinvent themselves before they are disrupted."[9]

Transformation requires leadership to rethink how their organizations create value today and tomorrow. Transformation starts with strategy, drives the creation of new business and care models, explores new relationships with customers, builds new competencies and capabilities, and delivers new efficiencies and more. Incremental improvement is not enough to win in today's competitive healthcare environment.

Transformation requires planning, designing, deploying, demonstrating, and creating value. According to Michael Porter, "Value should always be defined around the customer, and in a well-functioning health care system, the creation of value for patients should determine the rewards for all other actors in the system. Since value depends on results, not inputs, value in health care is measured by the outcomes achieved, not the volume of services delivered, and shifting focus from volume to value is a central challenge."[6] Transformation asks key questions, including

- What business are we in—and why?
- Who do we do business with—and why?
- What growth opportunities exist?
- How can we reinvent care processes?
- How can we deliver new efficiencies?

The transformation of a healthcare enterprise, market, or ecosystem requires a profound major change in strategies, leadership, organization structures, operating models, capabilities, and measures of success. Today and tomorrow, digital technologies, such as mobile, social, analytics, and the cloud, will complement EHRs and current enterprise systems to address real problems within the enterprise, and across the extended enterprise, with partners and affiliates. New business models and care models will produce innovations in consumer and patient experience, health and wellness, clinical service lines, etc. While the terms are often used synonymously, innovation and transformation are very different. In his *Forbes* article, "Innovation Vs. Transformation: The Difference in a Digital World," Daniel Newman states, "One of the major differentiating factors between transformation and innovation is speed—or lack thereof. Transformations take time—moving from one state to another is a process. Innovation usually refers to a sudden spark or creativity…the start of something great, what happens after is transformation."[10] For the purposes of this book, we will use the term transformation to represent all forms of significant change, including innovation.

Preparing for Tomorrow: Rationalizing Demand

Three complementary business investment categories—run the business, grow the business, and transform the business—provide a simple framework for prioritizing spending within the IT portfolio. While these three categories are not measures of value, they do help healthcare leaders compare IT investments and are defined as

- *Run the Business*: Providing consistent quality services for "keep the lights on" activities of the traditional healthcare enterprise and improving price-to-performance ratios while reducing cost and risk.
- *Grow the Business*: Improving revenue generation potential of existing business models through improvement or expanded market capacity.

■ *Transform the Business*: Radically changing business and care models, the processes that deliver them, the organizational capabilities and competencies, and the markets and customers served.[11]

Unfortunately, for many healthcare organizations, more than 80% of the IT function's efforts focus on run the business activities or activities of the traditional healthcare enterprise—often hospital care. In their report, "2017 State of Cost Transformation in U.S. Hospitals: An Urgent Call to Accelerate Action," Kaufman Hall observes that "Most hospitals and health systems…will require an extensive effort to dramatically lower costs by 25%–30% over a five-year period."[12] Today, in this country, 32 cents of every healthcare dollar is spent on hospital care. Better homecare options, largely made possible by digital health innovations, telemedicine, and new payment structures, will keep many patients out of the hospital. We will begin to see the de-hospitalization of the healthcare industry.[13] Most organizations will have to make a dramatic shift in their strategic priorities and the distribution of IT work between run, grow, and transform activities (Figure 3.1).

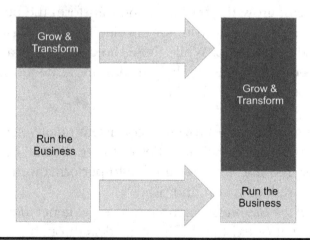

Figure 3.1   The strategic shift.[14]

For most health systems, an IT Demand Rationalization process is in order. The purpose of Demand Rationalization is to maximize the value of investments in IT, synchronize IT strategies with overall business strategies, reduce cost and complexity, and pave the way for grow and transform initiatives. Demand Rationalization requires a critical assessment of the IT and business workload required in run, grow, and transform activities and asks key questions, such as

- Are we doing the right things?
- Are we doing them the right way?
- Are we doing them for the right reason?
- Are we getting the right results?

Detailed examination of the IT portfolio, including strategies, applications, infrastructure, projects, services, corporate versus localized resources, vendor relationships, etc., will identify opportunities to divest and streamline specific "keep the lights on" activities. Leaders may decide to launch a Demand Rationalization effort in conjunction with a merger or consolidation effort during the strategic planning process, as part of a review of corporate services or IT operations, during the annual budget process, or in order to free up resources to support grow and transform initiatives.

Yet IT, traditionally a health-system expense center, has been viewed as a "cost of doing business." Senior executives must defend IT requests and justify spending as part of the annual budget process. By contrast, a strategic grow or transform program or project focuses on long-term change, often over many years' time. Often viewed as a strategic investment that will produce specific value, results, and outcomes, long-term ROI is essential. This type of strategic demand focusing on new markets, new services, new value-based care contracts, new enterprise strategies such as population health management, and new partnerships and affiliations should gradually replace initiatives and projects that focus on the traditional hospital or acute-care business.

Tomorrow: New Levels of Transformation

In the past 10 years, the role of information and technology within the healthcare industry has made dramatic leaps. Initially implemented within single entities, systems were single purposed, and they were generally designed to automate hospital departments such as nursing care, laboratory, revenue management, pharmacy, materials management, physician practice management, and clinical documentation. With a proliferation of vendors to meet specific niche functions, workarounds and manual processes still existed with limited information exchange across these proprietary systems. Over time, an integrated approach led by many large health systems sought to deploy one enterprise vendor across acute and ambulatory sites. As the industry consolidated, with health systems acquiring practices and merging with each other, IT has been used to standardize cross-continuum and cross-geography processes to drive efficiency-reducing costs. Transformation, however, was still focused on existing healthcare enterprises and processes (Figure 3.2).

In the coming years, digital transformation and innovation will drive value through

■ *The Extended Enterprise*: Loosely coupled, self-organizing networks of healthcare providers, payers, and adjacent companies that combine their capital, expertise, and customer base to achieve outcomes together that they could not do alone. Often focused on some aspect of the value chain, firms in the extended enterprise may operate independently or cooperatively through agreements and contracts. Examples today include clinically integrated

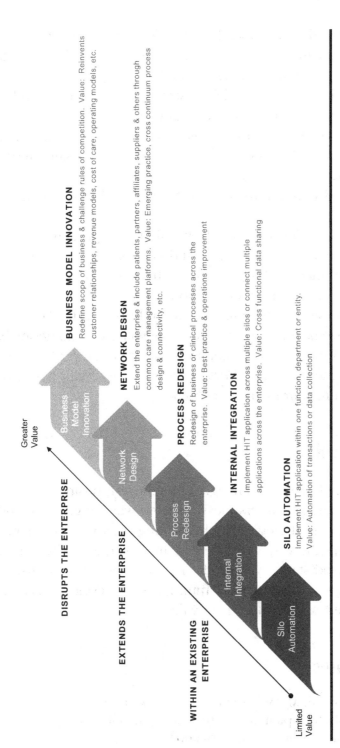

Figure 3.2 Levels of transformation.

networks, accountable care organizations, health-information organizations, joint ventures, alliances, etc.

■ *New Operating Models*: Team-based, patient-centric, connected care models designed using evidence and data to inform care processes will replace our historic hospital-focused care-delivery system. Dyad leadership models, using well-defined outcome metrics, will design emerging practices and collaborate with employed and affiliated physicians and their teams to create value and manage risks.

■ *New Business Models*: New value through new connections with health and healthcare consumers will impact all aspects of the healthcare industry from prevention and wellness to management of chronic disease and to palliative and end-of-life care. The movement away from sick care will create solutions based on innovative combinations of new value propositions, payment and reimbursement, ways of working together, and resources and capabilities.

Conclusion

If IT is to become a strategic differentiator, business, clinical, and IT leaders must clear the way for growing and transforming strategies. By harnessing collaborative energies to rethink the way work is performed, value will become the natural end state. Every dollar invested should be focused on building the organization's future, driving results and desired outcomes, and creating new value.

Endnotes

1. Morrison, M. "What Is Business Transformation?" RapidBI. September 5, 2012. https://rapidbi.com/what-is-business-transformation-3/.

2. "What Are the Advantages of Electronic Health Records?" HealthIT.gov. Accessed August 6, 2018. https://www.healthit. gov/faq/what-are-advantages-electronic-health-records.

3. Cohen, J. K. "61% of Healthcare Officials Indicate Terrible, Poor ROI on EHRs, Survey Finds." Becker's Hospital Review. September 18, 2017. https://www.beckershospitalreview.com/ ehrs/61-of-healthcare-officials-indicate-terrible-poor-roi-on-ehrs-survey-finds.html.

4. Bowman, S. "Impact of Electronic Health Record Systems on Information Integrity: Quality and Safety Implications." Perspectives in Health Information Management. October 1, 2013. https://www.ncbi.nlm.nih.gov/pmc/articles/PMC3797550/.

5. Arnold, S. ed. *Guide to the Electronic Medical Practice Strategies to Succeed, Pitfalls to Avoid.* Chicago: HIMSS, 2007.

6. Porter, M. E. "What Is Value in Health Care?" *New England Journal of Medicine* 363, No. 26 (2010): 2477–2481. doi:10.1056/ nejmp1011024.

7. Christensen, C. M. "Will Disruptive Innovations Cure Health Care?" *Harvard Business Review.* August 1, 2014. https://hbr. org/2000/09/will-disruptive-innovations-cure-health-care.

8. O'Riordan, A. and J. Elton. "Disruptive Forces Driving a New Order in Healthcare Business Models." Pharmaceutical Executive Home. October 31, 2017. http://www.pharmexec.com/ disruptive-forces-driving-new-order-healthcare-business-models.

9. Main, M., J. Weiss, and S. Blanchard. "The Healthcare CEO Gets a New Job." 2016. www.accenture.com.

10. Newman, D. "Innovation Vs. Transformation: The Difference In A Digital World." *Forbes.* May 4, 2017. https://www.forbes.com/sites/danielnewman/2017/02/16/ innovation-vs-transformation-the-difference-in-a-digital-world/.

11. Hunter, R. et al. "A Simple Framework to Translate IT Benefits Into Business Value Impact." Gartner Inc. May 16, 2008.

12. "2017 State of Cost Transformation in U.S. Hospitals: An Urgent Call to Accelerate Action." 2017. https://www.kaufmanhall.com/ sites/default/files/2017-State-of-Cost-Transformation-in-U.S.-Hospitals.pdf.

13. Leaf, C. "2 Forces That Will Drive the Health Industry." *Fortune.* Accessed August 6, 2018. http://fortune.com/2018/01/03/ health-care-industry-2018/.

14. Bell, S. *Run Grow Transform: Integrating Business and Lean IT.* Boca Raton: CRC Press, Taylor & Francis Group, 2013.

Chapter 4

The Value Management Framework: A Foundation for Systems Thinking

Purpose

To explore a systems thinking approach to rapidly assess the ROI and value opportunities associated with a program or project and to understand a framework for developing the Transformation Road Map.

In this chapter, the reader will learn to

- Recognize silver-bullet or linear thinking
- Understand why a systems thinking approach is preferred for today's complex healthcare environment
- Examine the steps in completing a Rapid ROI and Value Assessment
- Set the stage for the hard work ahead, developing the Transformation Road Map

Different Thinking

Information technology has often been cast as the *silver bullet* for a variety of healthcare's challenges. In Western literature, the phrase refers to an action which cuts through complexity and provides an immediate solution to a giant problem. The fictional hero the Lone Ranger popularized the allusion of a miraculous fix. In this radio-television series, silver bullets fit well with the masked hero's miraculous persona. He typically arrived from nowhere, overcame evil, and departed, leaving behind only a silver bullet and echoes of "who was that masked man?"[1] Today, silver bullets describe the next big change in an organization's tools, resources, or processes that will singularly perform a miracle and solve the health system's problems. As in the case of EHRs, we know this assumption is erroneous.

Silver-bullet thinking is a type of linear thinking or cause-and-effect thinking. Healthcare leaders often make decisions in a sequential manner—if I implement this system, it will solve this problem; if I train this doctor, he will become a more proficient EHR user; if I analyze these data, I will get these answers; etc. This type of thinking, at best, results in a limited return on investment. At worst, budgets are overrun due to unanticipated costs, timelines are exceeded due to unknown requirements, and/or unintended consequences abound.

Well documented in the healthcare industry literature, the Office of the National Coordinator for HIT (ONC), in conjunction with the Agency for Health Research and Quality (AHRQ), provides examples of the most common unintended consequences, including

- More work for clinicians
- Unfavorable workflow changes
- Conflicts between the computer and paper-based systems
- Unfavorable changes in communication practices and patterns
- Never-ending demands for system changes

- Negative user emotions
- Generation of new kinds of errors
- Unexpected changes in institutional power structure
- Overdependence on technology

Unintended consequences potentially undermine provider acceptance, result in increased costs, sometimes lead to failed implementation, and can even result in harm to patients.[2]

Today's healthcare executives oversee a portfolio of hospitals, employed and affiliated physician groups, diagnostic and post-acute services, community partnerships, contracts with payers, retail health providers and employers, services distributed across broad geographies, and now with the growth of telehealth, virtual services to patients near and far. No two health systems are the same, and the structures, relationships, and agreements that make up each health system's portfolio change continuously. In a simpler time during the year 2002, the father of modern management, Peter Drucker, said, "Health care is the most difficult, chaotic and complex industry to manage today."[3] Linear thinking does not work in this complex environment.

Systems thinking is a growing discipline designed to tackle complexity and produce significant results as we change healthcare practices, processes, technologies, organizations, reimbursement, and business models. It is a structured approach that emphasizes examining problems more completely and accurately before developing and implementing solutions. Systems thinking, as defined by Peter Senge, focuses on

- The organization as a whole
- Interactions between parts, not the parts themselves
- The way systems affect other systems
- Reoccurring patterns rather than just individual events
- Change over time
- How feedback affects the parts[4]

Systems thinking allows us to more effectively examine complexities. It also allows us to experiment, learn, and understand how we think about a problem. Systems thinking encourages a holistic understanding of the enterprise and takes a longer view of change. Rather than quick fixes, it focuses on identifying the root causes instead of working on symptoms, creating shared understanding of the factors influencing a problem, and working together as part of multidisciplinary teams to solve problems. Systems thinking prioritizes specific value levers and measures the level of change over time. Rather than in-depth, time-consuming analysis and preparation and planning for all these factors, a practical, agile approach for investigation and evaluation of options for value realization and/or creation is recommended.

Rapid ROI and Value Assessment

Leadership teams should start by quickly evaluating value realization and/or creation opportunities within their organization. The Rapid ROI and Value Assessment provides a framework as seen in Figure 4.1 for a high-level

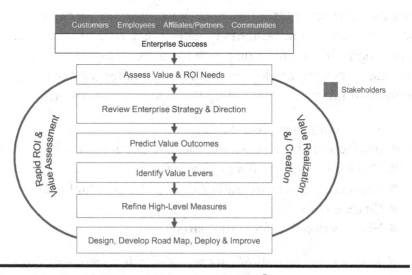

Figure 4.1   Rapid ROI and Value Assessment.[5]

opportunity-assessment process. The approach starts by briefly assessing the value needs of key stakeholders, individually, in groups, across the enterprise, and with key partners and affiliates. This process is not meant to be a detailed review of options. It can be completed through advanced preparation and a few short meetings (a couple of hours each) of key clinical, financial, data, and technology stakeholders. The process is illustrated below, and each component is described with examples in the following paragraphs.

Assess Value and ROI Needs

Value and ROI needs for each stakeholder group should be identified at a high level. While most organizations focus on their strategic plan to identify priorities, additional input may also be useful. The health system's Quality Plan is a valuable guide for brainstorming specific opportunities for improvement. If one does not exist, AHRQ has identified six domains of quality that are generally applicable in supporting the key stakeholders of a healthcare organization:

- *Safe*: Avoiding harm to patients from the care that is intended to help them.
- *Effective*: Providing services based on scientific knowledge to all who could benefit and refraining from providing services to those not likely to benefit (avoiding underuse and misuse, respectively).
- *Patient-centered*: Providing care that is respectful of and responsive to individual patient preferences, needs, and values, ensuring that patient values guide all clinical decisions.
- *Timely*: Reducing waits and sometimes harmful delays for both those who receive and those who give care.
- *Efficient*: Avoiding waste, including waste of equipment, supplies, ideas, and energy.

■ *Equitable*: Providing care that does not vary in quality because of personal characteristics such as gender, ethnicity, geographic location, and socioeconomic status.[6]

Simultaneously, enterprise financial metrics such as profitability, liquidity, cost, revenue, capital, and utilization should also be considered. In a 2017 systematic literature review, Barnes, Oner, Ray, and Zengal concluded there is a "relationship between the six domains of healthcare quality and improved financial performance. For example, providing safe care improved case flow with lower nursing-related adverse events. Further, there was a higher likelihood of adverse patient safety events in organizations with lower margins."[7] In other words, focusing on quality could improve financial results and vice versa.

The ROI and value requirements for stakeholder groups and the enterprise should be strategic yet specific. For example, patients are a subgroup of customers. Over time, value to patients will improve if we move them from engaged patients to activated patients. Engaged patients are open to learning about their health and chronic conditions. They are willing to answer questions about preferred treatment, and during direct patient care encounters, they make decisions with their providers based on medical evidence, clinical judgement, and their preferences. Patient activation takes patient participation in their health and healthcare one step further. It refers to patients with the skills, ability, and willingness to manage their own health and healthcare. Numerous studies have indicated that improved patient activation levels produce value (i.e., improved health outcomes and patient experience), as well as improved financial performance for the organization.[8]

Review Enterprise Strategy and Direction

Given the dynamic nature of today's healthcare environment, strategic plans and initiatives are constantly changing. It is essential for healthcare leaders to compare the value needs identified in the first step of the assessment with enterprise strategy and direction and map the value needs with associated strategies. For example, during 2018, CMS Administrator Seema Verma said in a speech at the Commonwealth Club of California, "CMS's Central mission is to transform the health care delivery system to one that moves away from delivering volume of services to one that delivers value for patients—one that provides high quality accessible care, at the lowest cost, and while many that have come before me have shared this vision, what is different now, is how we get there. By creating measures that allow providers to focus on the patient and help patients take ownership of their own care, CMS will be able to deliver on the promise of patient-centered healthcare." Given this focus by CMS, more health systems will shift more of their efforts toward patient engagement strategies and develop programs to address the specific needs of these key stakeholders.[9]

Predict Value Outcomes and Identify Value Levers

A variety of methods, including industry research, lessons learned, benchmarking the experience of others, etc., can identify a variety of potential outcomes or results of specific value levers. Value levers are defined as actions that can be taken to affect change. For most, the number of leverage points or things they can do to impact performance is limitless. Approaches such as the 80/20 rule and high-level data analysis can help identify a group of prioritized levers. Potential value levers exist in a variety of settings such as the workplace, hospitals, disease management programs, the community, and primary care. Examples of those value levers include health coaching, education, home monitoring, wearables, care protocols, portals, etc.

Refine High-Level Measures

Value measures should be developed and tracked in near real time over the life of the initiative or program. For some, metrics will be required as part of value-based contracts with payers; for others, they will be part of regulatory reporting; and for each organization, there will be some measures that are part of internal dashboards and unique to the health system. In our patient activation example, the Patient Activation Measure (PAM) that links activation levels to health outcomes, costs, and patients' experiences of care could quickly be identified as a predictor. The PAM has proven to be reliable and valid across different languages, cultures, demographic groups, and health statuses. The PAM is a latent construct—a variable that can't be measured directly but instead is assessed through a series of answers to questions—that gauges a person's self-concept as a manager of his or her health and healthcare. The measure is scored on a 0–100 scale, and people are categorized into four levels of activation, with level 1 the least activated and level 4 the most activated.[10]

Design, Develop Transformation Road Map, Execute, and Improve

Once the Rapid ROI and Value Assessment is complete, the organization will have a directional focus that allows them to begin the more detailed plan for transformation, ongoing ROI, and value realization and creation. The real work begins! The remainder of this chapter provides an overview of the Transformation Road Map.

The Hard Work of Transformation: Developing the Road Map

As stated in the first book in this series, "Value must be managed into reality through a multi-stage plan that identifies anticipated tangible and intangible value, accountable person or teams, and the steps to manage value over the entire life cycle of the initiative."[11] Many silver-bullet thinkers see the IT implementation or selecting a system as the primary focus of their efforts. In today's tight budget environment, they must also consider *why* they need the technology and go beyond selection and justification planning. In addition to the *why*, leadership must also consider the details of the *what, how, who, when*, and the relationship between the business and clinical components of the project, including organization structure and operating model, process, data, change management, culture, etc. The Transformation Road Map defines three important stages of *managing the value into reality*, including

- *Enterprise portfolio management*: Governance, Transformation Program Management, and the Investment Management Process. These components are discussed in Chapters 5 and 6.
- *The value management plan*: Strategy, Value Levers, Degree of Change, and Agile Iterations. This plan is addressed in Chapter 7.
- *Ongoing portfolio measurement*: ROI and Value Measurement and The Transformation Scorecard are explored in Chapters 8 and 9, respectively.

Figure 4.2 introduces the Transformation Road Map.

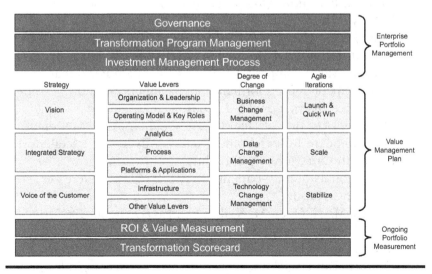

Figure 4.2   The Transformation Road Map.

Conclusion

Systems thinking provides a holistic approach to planning for and managing the value of a transformation initiative into reality. Rather than jumping into detailed planning for a major program or project, it is helpful to quickly assess the ROI and value opportunities, as well as the organization's ability to measure the impact of change. Having introduced the Transformation Road Map, the following chapters will take the reader through the more detailed steps, including enterprise portfolio planning, individual program planning, and portfolio measurement.

Endnotes

1. Martin, G. "'Silver Bullet' - the Meaning and Origin of This Phrase." *Phrasefinder*, www.phrases.org.uk/meanings/silver-bullet.html.
2. "Module I: Introduction to Unintended Consequences." HealthIT.gov. Accessed August 17, 2018. https://www.healthit.gov/unintended-consequences/content/module-i-introduction-unintended-consequences.html.
3. Drucker, P. F. *Managing in the Next Society.* Oxford: Butterworth-Heinemann, 2002.
4. Senge, P. M. *The Fifth Discipline: The Art and Practice of the Learning Organization.* New York: Doubleday, 1990.
5. Jack, A. "Value Mapping-A Second Generation Performance Measurement and Performance Management Solution." Business Excellence International Ltd., 2001.
6. "The Six Domains of Health Care Quality." AHRQ–Agency for Healthcare Research and Quality: Advancing Excellence in Health Care. July 17, 2015. https://www.ahrq.gov/professionals/quality-patient-safety/talkingquality/create/sixdomains.html.
7. Barnes, M., N. Oner, M. N. Ray, and F. D. Zengul. "Exploring the Association between Quality and Financial Performance in U.S. Hospitals: A Systematic Review." *Journal of Health Care Finance.* Fall 2017. http://healthfinancejournal.com/index.php/johcf/article/view/144.

8. James, J. "Patient Engagement." Health Policy Brief: Patient Engagement. February 14, 2013. https://www.healthaffairs.org/do/10.1377/hpb20130214.898775/full/.

9. Heath, S. "Verma: CMS Makes Strides in Patient-Centered Care, Medicare Reform." Patient Engagement HIT. July 26, 2018. https://patientengagementhit.com/news/verma-cms-makes-strides-in-patient-centered-care-medicare-reform.

10. Ibid.

11. Arlotto, P. and J. Oakes. *Return on Investment: Maximizing the Value of Healthcare Information Technology.* Chicago, IL: Healthcare Information and Management Systems Society, 2003.

Chapter 5

Transformation Governance: An Integrated Approach to Decision-Making

Purpose

To describe a new model and structure for integrated decision-making.

In this chapter, the reader will learn to

- Define governance as it relates to healthcare transformation
- Understand the difference in corporate governance and transformation governance
- Explore the responsibilities of governance versus leadership
- Describe how a Transformation Management Office (TMO) can play an integral role in the transition from volume to value

Transformation Governance: A New Model

As the velocity of change in healthcare accelerates, traditional decision-making structures no longer support the complexity, scope, risk, and expense associated with the transformative nature of today's information and technology platforms. As a mission-critical strategic asset that touches all we do in health and healthcare, IT can no longer be managed separately as a function, department, or division. In the past, health systems created IT steering committees to address system implementations and support ongoing maintenance of *run-the-business* IT applications. Physician advisory groups were established to provide input to EHR implementations in acute-care and ambulatory settings. Every three to five years, healthcare leaders created enterprise strategic plans. In response, IT would craft IT strategic plans and map key technology strategies back to the broader enterprise strategy to provide alignment. In recent years, new thinking regarding IT's role as part of the strategic planning process has emerged. As we move from 1.0 brick-and-mortar healthcare, to the 2.0 transition, and then to 3.0 digital health and connected care, IT strategies and investments should be integrated with business plans to focus on the *change-the-business* strategies of growth and transformation. IT must be governed as a component of the enterprise, not as a siloed function delegated solely to the chief information officer (CIO) or IT department.

As mentioned in previous sections of this book, integrated decision-making between HIT and other leadership team members is an essential part of value realization and creation. As the change to value-based care and other disruptions occur, traditional operational leadership teams will focus on running the traditional business. New governance structures must be put in place to recognize the impact, balance decisions, and ensure proper management of investments in transformational initiatives. Initially, transformation activities may be limited,

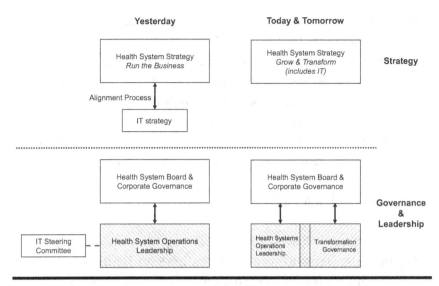

Figure 5.1   Changing strategy and governance & leadership models.

and depending on the size of the organization, the overlap in membership and focus will vary. Over time, as the degree of change accelerates traditional operations, leadership and transformation governance may become one and the same. Figure 5.1 depicts both the change in strategy and the change in governance and leadership.

Governance is

- A component of the overall corporate strategy and governance process
- Responsible for a holistic oversight process that crosses the entire value chain
- Led by the most senior decision-makers of the organization, those involved in the big-bet decisions of the enterprise: How fast will we transition from volume to value? Who are our partners and affiliates? What new business models (i.e., patient-centered medical homes, clinical integration networks, accountable care organizations, etc.) are we deploying? How much are we willing to invest in transformation and innovation? Who has the expertise and should be at the table?

■ Accountable for the answers to key questions: What is our vision for the future? Who makes decisions? Who has input? What are our top strategies and programs? Who is responsible for key initiatives, and who is consulted? How do we balance our legacy technologies with new innovative solutions? What is our philosophy regarding risk management, standardization, cost, timing, and value? Are we managing IT as an asset or a cost center?

In contrast, leadership supports governance by

■ Developing program and project portfolio management tools
■ Collaborating with business partners and affiliates across the continuum and departmental/divisional lines to share data and information with each other
■ Managing talent, application, architecture, infrastructure, and sourcing strategies
■ Supporting data and analytics, informatics, and quality initiatives
■ Maintaining service and operational levels that promote continuous business-IT alignment
■ Identifying emerging trends and new technologies and educating governance on potential impact to the enterprise
■ Answering questions for transformation initiatives: What is the business case? What is the as-is and to-be? To whom do we communicate? How do we measure success? How do we plan? How do we reward success?

Figure 5.2 illustrates the difference in governance and leadership roles.

In recent years, the classic critique of IT by healthcare business executives is as follows:

■ IT is not responsive to the business
■ IT does not understand our requirements

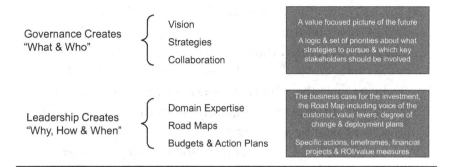

Figure 5.2   Governance v. leadership roles.

■ IT is too slow to deliver
■ The costs are too high
■ Quality is low[1]

The reality is that within a siloed operating model and governance structure, IT is challenged to keep up with the exponential level of change that is happening in healthcare. Though business and clinical leaders may occasionally team up with IT project managers, analysts, and applications specialists, ongoing results-oriented collaboration is rare. Integrated governance models can help take IT-business collaboration to the next level. In an environment where rapid-fire innovation, new business and care models, and new technologies can render traditional processes, roles, and tools obsolete, new *change-the-business* governance models are essential.

There is no single model for governance in today's healthcare organization, yet there are several emerging trends that should be considered in the design:

■ HIT and digital tools touch every part of the enterprise and the extended enterprise today and can no longer be governed with an IT-focused steering committee or governance structure.
■ The senior most decision-makers of the organization should make up the transformation governance group and drive transformational strategies.

■ For most health-system boards, new challenges arise in overseeing the transition from volume to value. Even the most seasoned directors have gaps when it comes to keeping up with the challenges facing the healthcare industry and the expertise needed to use analytics, new platforms of care, and digital tools to drive new models of care and healthcare business.

■ Given the breadth and depth of the change, the health-system board should be informed and educated. New board members with experience in data and technology can influence transformation strategy and governance direction.

■ Transformation leadership cannot be integrated into the day-to-day activities of operations. While some organizations name a chief transformation or innovation officer, the responsibilities can be handled by a chief information officer (CIO), chief medical informatics officer (CMIO), chief medical officer (CMO), chief operations officer (COO), etc. Leadership skills are more important than subject-matter expertise.

■ Transformation governance generally composed of *change-the-business* leadership will report to the corporate board, partner with operational leaders, and work with integrated project teams as seen in Figure 5.3 to orchestrate the change effort. Services such as IT, informatics, analytics, quality, and others provide the necessary domain expertise to support the program and projects.

■ Governance structures and processes should be defined based on the culture, capabilities, and progress the organization is making toward value-based care.

■ Transformational strategies will vary by organization and be prioritized based on investment required and objectives for ROI/value. From a systems thinking perspective, transformation governance should be designed to incorporate the multiple levels of the enterprise decision making, internally and externally. Figure 5.3 summarizes the various levels of the organization governance should oversee.

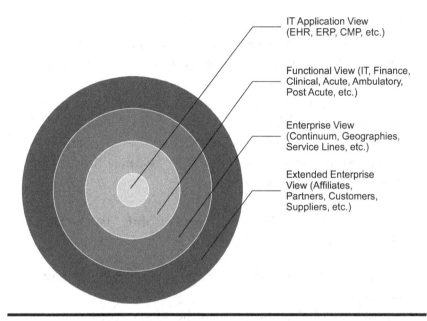

IT Application View
(EHR, ERP, CMP, etc.)

Functional View (IT, Finance,
Clinical, Acute, Ambulatory,
Post Acute, etc.)

Enterprise View
(Continuum, Geographies,
Service Lines, etc.)

Extended Enterprise
View (Affiliates,
Partners, Customers,
Suppliers, etc.)

Figure 5.3   Levels of the enterprise.

The Transformation Management Office (TMO)

An Enterprise Transformation Management Office (TMO) is defined as the central point of coordination for all transformation programs and projects. The central task of the TMO is to orchestrate the complex, often disruptive, change typically needed to achieve breakthrough value in transformation. The traditional project management office (PMO), focused on administration and compliance, is poorly suited to the pursuit of the value realization and creation opportunities presented by a transformation initiative.[2]

The TMO performs three indispensable roles as part of the transformation effort, including

■ In conjunction with the chief transformation officer or designated change officer, the TMO takes the lead in generating ideas for creating and realizing value, constantly re-energizing and re-focusing the transformation effort.

- Carries out the rigorous ROI/value assessment work to confirm that all investments (people, process, data, technology, change, etc.) are in sync and contributing to the transformation of business and care-management models.
- Does not regard compliance as its main objective and operates from a high-performance, agile operating model in which transformation programs and projects are designed, deployed, and refined in the most timely and cost-effective way possible.

While the TMO builds on the concept of the PMO, there are additional differences. The TMO

- Exists to transform clinical practice, not just to manage projects
- Facilitates collaboration across the silos of the health system and its partners, not just IT
- Moves beyond best practices to focus on emerging practices
- Challenges existing organizational structures and business models

Similarities between the role of the TMO and PMO are that they both

- Provide systematic processes and tools for reporting, milestone reviews, integrated work and resource planning, scheduling, change management, and active risk and issue management
- Ensure consistent and efficient program and project execution
- Support and provide governance information for decision-making

In the initial stages of the transformation effort, a number of important decisions must be made to ensure the most appropriate design of the TMO. Some of the decisions are

- Does the TMO integrate with existing committees, or is a separate structure needed?
- Are new roles, titles, and responsibilities needed for success?
- What will be the reporting process?
- What are the responsibilities and authorities of the TMO: facilitator or watchdog?
- Who has the final say regarding resources, priorities, and workflow decisions?
- Should an escalation process be defined in advance in case groups or individuals have difficulty making decisions?
- What education and training methods will be used?
- Should existing project management and process redesign capabilities be augmented?
- What tools will team members need (e.g., status reporting, issue management, risk identification, project budget management, milestone tracking, project charters, executive dashboards)?
- How will communications occur and how frequently?
- Are new incentives needed for dedicated team members or physician participants?

The TMO is a vital component of a health system's strategy to transform clinical practice. Opportunities exist to become more efficient, more effective, and to reinvent the patient's journey.

Conclusion

Governance, decision-making, and supporting structures are critical to the success of transformation initiatives. While governance, leadership, and program management roles may vary by organization, practical results will require attention to the details described within this chapter. In the next chapter, readers will begin to explore the more detailed investment management process.

Endnotes

1. https://www-935.ibm.com/services/multimedia/A_new_era_begins_Avril_2013.pdf
2. Forrest, C. "Do You Need a Transformation Management Office?" CIO. August 21, 2018. https://www.cio.com.au/article/552697/do_need_transformation_management_office_/.

Chapter 6

Making the Case for Investment: Setting the Stage with an Investment-Management Process

Purpose

To set the stage for the enterprise investment-management process to help evaluate and prioritize transformation programs and IT projects.

In this chapter, the reader will learn to

- Define the transition from budget management to investment management
- Understand the bottom-up and top-down approaches to planning
- Explore methods for prioritizing projects, programs, and portfolios
- Identify value levers that may impact programs and projects

From Budget Management to Investment Management

Every organization must make decisions about IT investment (see Figure 6.1). In some organizations, the process is informal with only a few key decision-makers. Other health systems use analytic tools as supporting documentation to help gain buy-in for a specific proposal. Yet in others, more rigorous methods move through a series of evaluation committees. The underlying question for all organizations should be: "Given limited dollars across the enterprise, how do we optimize our investment?" At a minimum, the chief information officer, chief financial officer, and chief strategy officer should work together to create an IT investment-management process. As health systems take on transformation programs and projects, integrated Road Maps that include detailed financial plans and payback periods for multiple value levers, including IT, will be necessary. The purpose of the investment process is to make the case for investment and prioritize expenditures given the changing environment and associated enterprise strategies.

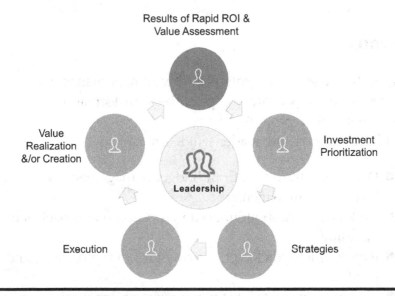

Figure 6.1   Decision-making cycle.

Ideally, the investment-management process

■ Recognizes the ROI and value realization and creation opportunities for the enterprise as identified in the Rapid ROI and Value Assessment process described in Chapter 4
■ Ensures that investments are integrated within the overall strategic plan of the enterprise
■ Clarifies the level of change: incremental, transformation, or targeted innovation
■ Begins with initial project identification, rolls-up projects to the program level, aggregates the programs into the broader strategic portfolio, includes required analyses for evaluation and prioritization, and continues over the life of the project
■ Is metric driven with clear goals
■ Includes checkpoints at appropriate intervals to make sure the organization is on track to achieve predetermined goals
■ Provides support in the form of tools, education, and benchmarks

The investment-management process should be integrated into the enterprise-strategic-planning process. As mentioned previously, IT plans should be embedded in the enterprise strategy and should not be included as separate plans. Rather than viewing IT as a cost of doing business, leadership should consider the multi-year implications and the opportunity for value realization and creation. As shown in Figure 6.2, the investment-management process includes both top-down and bottom-up planning.

Understanding the difference in the two planning approaches is important. Specifically, the top-down or enterprise approach allows for integration of IT investment requirements within the broader portfolio of strategic initiatives. As mentioned earlier, for many organizations, investments will focus on growth and transformation rather

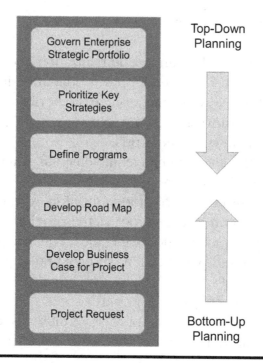

Figure 6.2 Investment management process.

than run the business or "keep-the-lights-on" activities. Examples include

■ Growth of a clinical integration network may need further investment in EHRs or interoperability.
■ Medicare shared savings program or commercial payer contracts may require investments in analytics.
■ Advanced population health-management strategies may require care-management tools.
■ Health systems moving from patient-engagement to patient-activation strategies may require investment in home monitoring, clinical call centers, telehealth, and a variety of other technologies that support the consumer, patient, and community.

The bottom-up or project-level approach addresses single projects that are not part of a broader program or strategy.

Projects that do not achieve basic standards for the ROI, business case match, executive sponsorship, etc. should be screened out during the investment-management process.

The investment-management process will vary from organization to organization. Typically, a well-designed process will specify the stages of the planning process, how a program or project enters the process, the levels of analysis required, and how priorities are established. Value levers are the actions organizations take to drive change and therefore value. These values are unique to the health system and impact the degree of formality, the level of review needed, and other aspects of the design. Table 6.1 illustrates a number of value levers an organization should consider in its investment-management process.

Bottom-Up or Project-Level Planning

Most healthcare organizations have hundreds of items on their capital budget wish list. IT represents a substantial number of the requests and projects in the pipeline. Individual IT projects should undergo a thorough evaluation process to set the stage for governance to make a final decision on the appropriate projects to fund. The primary purpose of this examination is to screen out the many projects that do not meet basic thresholds and reduce the number of projects subject to detailed review to a manageable level. The degree of rigor depends on the project—some represent small levels of capital investment and technical support while others are more complex and require a business case and detailed budget analysis. Large projects may require more formal analytics. Small projects should not be overburdened with unnecessary evaluation while large projects receive an extensive review of expected deliverables and a plan for managing risks. As outlined in Figure 6.3, a staged process for a project review with go/no-go decisions along the way will highlight valuable projects and weed out those not fitting enterprise or operational objectives.

Table 6.1 Levers That May Impact Value

Type of Factor	Consideration
Political or policy levers	• Desired level medical staff participation • Leadership decision-making structures
Regulatory requirements	• Stakeholder perspectives • Divided authority over decisions (e.g., medical school versus hospital, individual hospital versus health system)
Organizational levers	• Poorly defined or overly ambitious strategy • Misalignment or conflicting internal goals • Complex programs • Leadership, organization design, and operating model • Culture
Financial levers	• Yearly and multi-year budget cycles • Capital availability • Operating margin and performance
Data & information, analytic levers	• Availability of integrated data warehouses • Data visualization tools • Descriptive, diagnostic, predictive, prescriptive analytics capabilities • Trust in internal data: clinical, financial, business, etc. • Availability of external data: claims, social determinants of health
Business process levers	• Impact on existing processes • Performance improvement opportunities • Standardization • Business model innovation
Technology levers	• Rapid changes in technology • Standard versus nonstandard configuration • Scale and complexity • Care-management platform design • Application and infrastructure strategy

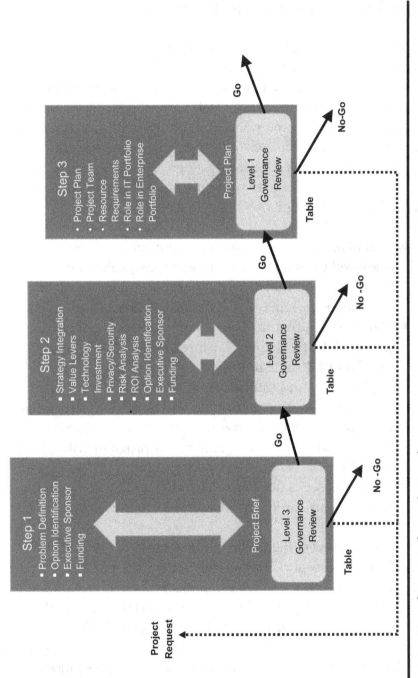

Figure 6.3 Staged process for project review.

Top-Down or Portfolio Planning

Most people manage their personal investment portfolios to get them to the point they wish to be at some future date, taking into account such factors as ROI and risk. Similarly, a portfolio of strategic programs will move the health system to a particular place at some point in the future. Individual projects are often bundled with related projects to create specific programs or initiatives. These programs are combined to create a portfolio of transformation programs. As shown in Figure 6.4, three important definitions help clarify each category:

- *Portfolio*: A suite of business or clinical programs managed to optimize overall enterprise value. During a transformation initiative, the portfolio should be defined as strategic programs, not just IT initiatives.
- *Program*: A structured grouping of projects designed to produce clearly defined business value. Major clinical and financial strategies often combine IT platforms, applications, and infrastructure with value levers such as design of new organization and leadership structures, operating models and roles, analytics-driven decision-making, processes, etc. Therefore, a program will typically be defined by its business purpose, not by IT application.
- *Project*: A set of activities delivering a defined capability based on an agreed-upon schedule and budget.

As mentioned earlier, a health system with a population health-management (PHM) strategy may have multiple programs consisting of multiple projects. Depending on the maturity of the program, the number of PHM contracts the enterprise has entered into, the level of sophistication of the organization's EHR and other systems, and the composition of these programs and projects may vary by organization. For more information on this topic, please refer to the book

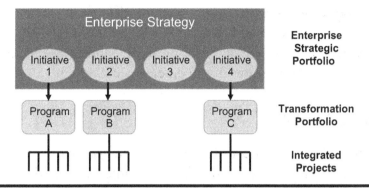

Figure 6.4   Portfolio planning.

Rethinking Return on Investment: The Challenge of Population Health Management, to be released in 2019.

A portfolio management approach that integrates IT within broader projects and programs, ensures review through multidisciplinary project teams, is owned by the business or clinical leaders, and is prioritized through the appropriate governance process should

- Change the organization's focus from cost to investment management
- Encourage more objective and transparent value analysis
- Improve resource allocation
- Balance strategic, routine, and mandatory initiatives
- Expand collaboration and communication

Investment Prioritization

While transformation programs and IT projects can be planned, the development of an investment prioritization plan is also important. As with other requests across the organization for both capital and operating funding, the number of requests usually far exceed both the resources available as well as the organizational bandwidth to implement the plans successfully.

A number of tools, including scoring models and arraying approaches, can be used to ensure appropriate grouping, comparison and prioritization of programs and projects, and strategic investments across the enterprise.

Scoring Models

Scoring models are most often used when comparing projects from a bottom-up perspective. As the name implies, the governance group, or project-selection committee, lists relevant criteria, such as

- *Strategic Impact*: To what degree does this IT project impact one or more stated enterprise strategic goals? Does this project have direct, measurable, and significant value on the transformation of care?
- *Clinical, Operational, and Strategic Information*: In what way does this project leverage or improve the data assets of the organization? How does it provide critical information for insight-driven decision making?
- *Regulatory Requirement*: Is the project required from a regulatory standpoint?
- *Risk*: How much risk is associated with this effort? To what degree have risks been identified and risk-mitigation plans developed?
- *ROI*: Has an ROI analysis been completed (see Chapter 8)? Does the analysis indicate a return that meets the enterprise's minimum requirements?
- *Technology Requirement*: Does the project support ongoing maintenance or upgrade of a key application or infrastructure?

Each criterion is weighted according to its importance and the organization's priorities. For example, 100 points may be spread across each criterion, and those with more importance are given more points. In the example given above, one health system may choose to give Strategic Impact and Clinical, Operational, and Strategic Information 30 points each, with the remaining 40 points spread equally across the remaining criteria. Each project is scored, and the projects with the highest scores are chosen.

Top-down planning and creation of enterprise strategic portfolios reduce the need for comparison of large numbers of single projects. For example, if the organization has elected to deploy virtual visits, one would ask how the proposed project fits into planned programs and the enterprise strategy. Virtual visits would be one project of many required to build out a Telehealth program and therefore would be part of a much larger patient activation strategy.

Arraying Approaches

The complete strategic portfolio of an enterprise will include a number of major programs, each containing specific projects. An arraying approach may help prioritize programs and the projects within them. The bubble diagram shown in Figure 6.5 is an ideal tool for ranking or "arraying" dimensions of value.

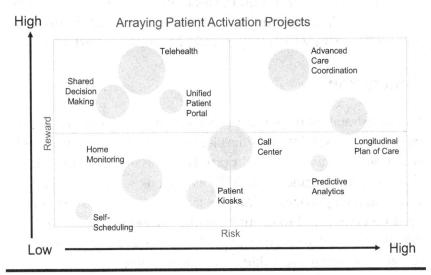

Figure 6.5 Arraying approaches.

Table 6.2   Arraying Approaches

X Axis	Y Axis	Bubble Size
Time to implement	Cost over life of project	Benefit over life of project
Ease of implementation	Organizational readiness	Cost of project
Strategic fit	Technological fit	Net present value

Using the criteria from the section above, one can assign both risk and reward (typically on a scale of 1–10), as well as quantify the magnitude of investment. As seen in Table 6.2, the "x" axis represents the risks associated with the program, the "y" axis the reward, and the "bubble" graphically indicates the size of the investment (large bubbles equate to larger investments while small bubbles equate to smaller investments). The Telehealth program previously mentioned has high value, low risk, and moderate investment requirements when compared with programs associated with patient engagement and activation. One may wish to use a series of bubble diagrams to address the various transformation programs within the organization.

On a higher level, program risks, rewards, and costs can be arrayed to help determine which programs should be funded and the order in which they should be implemented.

Conclusion

The investment-management process is broader than the annual budget process. It involves developing specific review practices at the project, program, and portfolio levels and may include using investment prioritization tools such as scoring models and arraying approaches. Various combinations of investments must be considered to ensure the organization is selecting initiatives that align with enterprise strategy and, given resource constraints, maximize value while minimizing risk.

Chapter 7

Managing Healthcare Information Technology as an Investment: The Value-Management Plan

Purpose

To move beyond justification to value-management planning, design, execution, and ongoing improvement.

In this chapter, the reader will learn to

- Organize and develop a Value-Management Plan
- Develop a Program Brief
- Document key value levers and the capacities required
- Define the degree of change and plan for deployment
- Communicate with key stakeholders

Planning Value into Reality

Historically, ROI, benefits realization, and value analysis have been used as tools for justification during the health system's annual budget process and are rarely referred to again. The question, "Did we achieve the project ROI or Value?" is not asked. Today, making the case for investment is only the first step. Healthcare leaders must manage the value into reality across several stages, including planning, design, execution, and ongoing improvement. Tight integration of business process redesign, new organizational structures and operating models, and information technology plans, along with disciplined change management, are necessary to ensure that value projections become reality.

A Value-Management Plan, providing an executive summary of the program and related projects, should be packaged in a clear, concise fashion. In addition to a clear rationale for investment, the Value-Management Plan should ensure integration of the organization's vision and program strategy, ensure the voice of the customer is heard, specify the value levers (those actions that must be taken to realize or create value), address the degree of change, and define the level of experimentation needed prior to scaling the new program or project across the enterprise. The Value-Management Plan will support understanding, as well as decision-making, for boards, steering committees, and other governing bodies through the entire life cycle of the effort and can serve as a

- Tool for education and expectation management
- Component of the enterprise and transformation-strategy process
- Proposal for use in the prioritization of resources and budgeting
- Set of milestones for use in program management as the initiative moves from initial concept through

evaluation, to implementation, and finally to ongoing improvement
■ Goal for metrics and score-carding

The Value-Management Plan is more than a business plan or a financial analysis. It is a dynamic document that contains the roadmap for creating shared understanding, definition, responsibilities, and actions for transformation programs and key IT projects. The Value-Management Plan is composed of the following:

■ The program/Project Brief
■ Desired value outcomes
■ Return on investment analysis (Chapter 8)
■ Key value levers and capabilities required
■ Definition of degree of change
■ Deployment plan
■ Communications plan
■ Value score card (Chapter 9)

The remainder of this chapter details the components of the Value-Management Plan. Chapters 8 and 9 go into more detail on ROI Analysis and Value Score Cards, respectively.

Starting Well: The Program/Project Brief

The Value-Management Plan should include a high-level summary or brief. The brief is typically a simple, preferably single-page, document completed by the Executive Sponsor. If the program is the result of top-down planning as described in Chapter 6, then the brief is created as a result of the strategic- or transformation-planning process. If it is bottom-up and is focused on a single IT project, it is created as part of the governance-review process. The brief is often the cover page for the more detailed aspects of the full Value-Management Plan and typically includes

- *Program/Project overview:* A summary of the purpose, background, scope, and key deliverables.
- *Team members:* Names, titles, contact information, and responsibilities of key stakeholders such as
  - *Executive sponsor (ES):* The most senior executive within the enterprise who is responsible for overall program success. The ES focuses on strategic value creation and/or realization and keeps these goals top of mind throughout the planning, design, and execution phases of the initiative. The ES ensures integration with health-system strategy, removes barriers, helps manage risks, and provides ongoing direction to the business owner(s) and the Transformation Management Office.
  - *Business owner(s) (BO):* The person accountable for business results and deployment of the value levers associated with the Value-Management Plan. The BO collaborates with others to ensure the desired future state is enabled by the program or project as defined.
  - *Other team members:* Project managers plus others, including IT, operations, clinicians, finance, etc.
- *The problem to be solved:* The primary purpose of the program and ultimate focus of the ES and BO. Problem definition typically requires research into the existing business or clinical environment and identification of the specific problem. Often addressed during the Rapid ROI and Value Assessment, organizational clarity, agreement on the problem, and potential combination of value levers help start the program well and increase the likelihood of success.
- *Impact on enterprise strategy:* Clear integration of the enterprise strategic direction and the role of the problem

to be solved, the solution presented as part of the program or project, and a summary of the desired value or expected outcomes.

Table 7.1 depicts an example of a Project Brief for a telehealth pilot project.

Desired Value Outcomes

Traditionally, IT program-management offices have been responsible for keeping IT projects on time, on budget, and on scope. In order to manage value into reality and start the project well, the Transformation Management Office (TMO), as described in Chapter 5, should work with Executive Sponsors and Business Owners to ensure that the desired value outcomes are clearly stated in the Value-Management Plan. For example, a number of potential desired outcomes for the telehealth program and its related virtual visits project could be identified during the Rapid ROI and Value Assessment phase, such as

- Make medical advice, diagnoses, and prescriptions for a range of conditions available remotely, without in-person visits
- Help remove barriers such as distance, traffic, and inflexible work hours—anything that can prevent or delay access to care
- Reduce risks of delayed care which can result in more serious, complex, and costly health conditions
- Make a connection with a medical professional available 24/7
- Drive better outcomes, such as 59% fewer hospital stays, 35% lower hospital admissions, and $2000 saved per patient per year[1]

Table 7.1 ABC Health System Project Brief

Project Name	TeleHealth Pilot
Executive Sponsor	Chief Population Health Officer
Business Owner	Vice President Population Health
Business Environment/ Problem to be Solved/ Objectives	Current capacity constraints with Primary Care and select specialties mean patients are either inappropriately utilizing the emergency department or are going out of the network to receive care. TeleHealth provides additional primary-care access points across the organization for patients to engage that will alleviate current bottlenecks, providing improved patient satisfaction.
Strategic Alignment	Telehealth aligns with one of our five strategic pillars: Consumer Engagement, and specifically is one of our key strategies for the coming year: develop TeleHealth strategy and pilot with a series of projects that will best impact our community.
Description	Pilot the use of TeleHealth services by providing non-urgent care access (e.g., sore throat, pink-eye) through the patient portal to enrolled patients. Additional infrastructure (video) will tie to the current EHR.
High-Level Requirements	Tele-capability between patients and designated providers to include phone and video. Specific providers are to be determined.
Assumptions	Can integrate into current EHR. Will be HIPAA compliant.

(Continued)

Table 7.1 (Continued)   ABC Health System Project Brief

Risks	Denial of claims, capacity
Process Impacted	Scheduling, Clinician Office Visit, Clinical Documentation, Billing, Care Coordination
Time Lines and Key Milestones (e.g., start and end date, duration)	Begin Implementation by April 1. Implementation and training will be complete for the start of the new fiscal year (October 1). Key Milestones: • Contract negotiation with hardware vendor by April 15 • Hardware implementation by June 15 • Software configuration by July 1 • Go live by September 1
High-Level Cost Estimate	Software: Already included with EHR Hardware: $67,000 for the server and monitors Installation/Training: $90,000 from the vendor Process Redesign: 450 hours from Process Improvement Incremental Staffing: 0.5 full-time-equivalents in the call center
Signature	John Hancock Betsy Ross Executive Sponsor Business Owner

■ Reduce in-person visits by 37%, 15%, and 15% of urgent care visits, emergency room visits, and office visits, respectively, as reported by Kaiser Permanente[2]

Another vital component clearly defining desired outcomes is to include the voice of the customer (VoC). This term, used in business and IT, describes the in-depth process of capturing customer's expectations, preferences, and aversions. Typically, VoC includes both quantitative and qualitative information that summarizes the customer's wants and needs, organized into a hierarchical structure and then prioritized in terms of relative importance and satisfaction. There are many ways to gather the information, including focus groups, surveys, individual interviews, etc.[3] Customers of virtual visits typically prioritize convenient access to care over face-to-face interaction. Typically, visits to the doctor's office average 37 minutes of travel time and 44 minutes of wait time to see a doctor for 20 minutes.[4] Using rigor similar to the ROI and financial analysis described in the next chapter, the analysis should include a definition of how the planned benefits will actually be realized and answers to the following questions:

■ Who will determine the timing for each step?
■ Who will be accountable for ensuring success?
■ What measures will demonstrate that the outcomes have been achieved?
■ How risks and critical success factors will be recognized?

Table 7.2 illustrates a more detailed summary of the desired outcomes as defined within a Value-Management Plan for virtual visits.

Key Value Levers and Capabilities Required

In Chapter 4, the term value lever is defined as the actions that can be taken to affect change. For ROI and Value

Table 7.2 Value Management Plan

Benefit	Goal/Desired Outcome	Documented Steps	Timeline	Responsible Parties	Metrics for Determining Success	Risks/Critical Success Factors
Additional volume/revenue due to Telehealth	Additional visit volume via virtual visits	• Deploy hardware necessary for telehealth • Create new visit types and associated charge codes	• 365 in year 1 • 1000 in year 2 • 5000 in year 3	Physicians Nursing Pharmacists	Number of virtual visits Net Revenue from virtual visits	• Physician buy-in • Revised workflow for virtual visits • Accurate billing and reimbursement
Improved patient access due to increased availability for face-to-face visits	Third next available appointment is less than two weeks	• Train call center staff on scheduling virtual visits • Conduct marketing campaign to promote virtual visits	• 25% in year 1 • 50% in year 2 • 75% in year 3	Call Center Information Technology Marketing	Average third next available appointment	• Call center training

(Continued)

Table 7.2 (Continued)   Value Management Plan

Benefit	Goal/Desired Outcome	Documented Steps	Timeline	Responsible Parties	Metrics for Determining Success	Risks/Critical Success Factors
Improved patient satisfaction around accessibility	Consumer assessment of healthcare providers & systems (CAHPS)scores around "Getting Timely Care, Appointments, and Information" 80% in "Always" box	• Activation of virtual visits • Promotion of virtual visits	• 70% in year 1 • 75% in year 2 • 80% in year 3	Patient Experience Officer	CAHPS scores around "Getting Timely Care, Appointments, and Information"	• Call center training • Quality of virtual visits

Realization or Creation to occur, IT must be coupled with strategy, organization and operations design, new operating models, analytics, process change, etc. Telehealth is a notable example of how technology implementation alone is not enough. Telemedicine technology began as a form of healthcare delivery in the late 1960s due to the needs of the National Aeronautics and Space Administration (NASA) and the Nebraska Psychology Institute. For the last 50 years, multiple barriers have stood in the way of widespread adoption, including financial, regulatory, care-delivery, and cultural challenges.[5] Today, however, a wide array of virtual-health and remote-monitoring applications are making significant differences in the transformation of healthcare. Overhaul of healthcare operating models and development of new capabilities, along with development of a robust roadmap for execution, is essential. For example, virtual visits require redesigning clinical workflows, enhancing scheduling capabilities, refining revenue management tools to handle reimbursements,[6] recruiting physicians to provide virtual consults, strengthening competencies of physicians, etc. Health systems may need foundational capabilities such as robust patient portals, self-service capabilities across multiple channels (including online, mobile, fixed line, and text messages), IT backbone and security, linkage to EHRs, etc. For each capability, the health system must determine whether to develop a sourcing strategy for all components—internal, outsourced, or through partnerships.[7] Other factors such as pricing models, compliance, and legal obligations are also key considerations. Planning for and integrating the design and the execution and management of value levers are as important, if not more important, than the technology decision. In the past, the healthcare industry has allowed the "technology tail to wag the dog" and expected ROI and value as a result.

Definition of Degree of Change

The Value-Management Plan will help clarify the level of change anticipated and underscore the scope of the initiative. Three levels of change are defined in Table 7.3.

The level of change will impact the desired deployment plan. Traditionally, IT initiatives such as EHRs and other enterprise applications were implemented with a big-bang implementation method. In other words, the entire system was turned on across the organization simultaneously on the same date. While the turnover was planned for months, sometimes years, in advance and the repercussions addressed for months afterwards, most major implementations were handled this way. Given the transformative nature of change today and the impact across multiple value levers, new deployment methods are needed.

Table 7.3   Scope of Change

Scope of Change	Impact	Definition
Innovation	Value creation	Targeted creation of new, more, or better value in a targeted fashion for a process, business model, or organizational capability.
Transformation	Combinations of value creation & realization	Large-scale enterprise change. May include some innovation coupled with design and deployment of new capabilities with large IT component. Often comprises significant cultural change.
Improvement	Value realization	Delivery on desired business or clinical outcomes through IT combined with other value levers.

Deployment Plans

The Care-Management Platform, as introduced in Chapter 2, and other cloud-based applications or "apps" comprise highly a configurable set of tools, services, and infrastructure. These platforms can be adapted based on the unique design of clinical workflows, end-user personalization, foundational systems, interoperability, clinical integration networks, commercial and governmental payer agreements, and other variables for each health system. These systems allow simultaneous standardization and configuration, rather than the customized feature-functionality of traditional IT modules. Instead of the big-bang deployments of the past, the platforms allow experimentation on a small scale. Change of business models, organization structures, process design, etc. can be deployed as a proof of concept. As the number of risk-based contracts move from a few thousand covered lives to significant numbers of attributed patients and populations, proven programs can be scaled and expanded.

As mentioned in previous chapters, Lean Startup and Agile models provide a set of principles for experimentation and achieving value while learning lessons quickly. In a nutshell, lean is focused on eliminating anything that doesn't add value. Lean puts a strong emphasis on what it calls "the system"—that is, the way the team operates as a whole. Lean shifts the focus to learning rather than implementing. Agile encourages iteration or rapid deployment of narrow components of the larger system.[8] Key factors for success include a focus on value backed up with transparency, collaboration, data-driven decision-making, fast/iterative deployment of technology-empowered processes, and simplicity. Hierarchy, command and control, complexity, and siloes become things of the past. Plans to launch, as part of a proof of concept with quick wins for specific customer groups to demonstrate value, followed by a roadmap to scale with further benefits realized, created and measured, and finally

Table 7.4 Cadence of Traditional IT Big-Bang v. Transformation Program Iteration

	Traditional IT Big Bang	Transformation Program Iteration
Scale	Enterprise-one time	Proof of concept & waves
Organization	Silos	Dedicated teams
Focus	IT implementation	Measurable value
Risk level	High-risk level	Non-event
Information	After-thought	Actionable
Culture	Do not fail	Fail fast, learning organization, continuous refinement
Schedule	One-time event	Focused micro events, continuous iterations
Metrics	On time, on budget	Qualitative and quantitative value, ROI
Key Result	Technology operational	New ways of working and improved outcomes
Cadence	Multi-year	Regular, predictive design and deployment leading to synchronization of multiple events happening at the same time as the program scales

specific steps toward stabilization should all be developed as part of the Value-Management Plan. Table 7.4 illustrates the cadence of transformation programs when compared to traditional IT big-bang implementations.

Communications and Expectation Management Plan

The Value-Management Plan should clarify the communication framework and document lessons learned along the way. This

Table 7.5   Communications Plan

Communication Purpose	Communication Vehicle	Responsible Parties
Weekly status reports	Redesign meetings	TMO Director Program Team Leads Clinical, Business, and Financial Work Groups
News and updates	Transformation newsletter	TMO Communications Analyst
Issues and resolution plan	Issues tracking list	TMO Director Executive Sponsor Business Owner(s) Program/Project Team Leads
Lessons learned from the industry	Transformation governance	TMO Process Consultants

plan will help the organization manage expectations and risks. Components should include

- Formal status reporting
- Grapevine management
- Problem management
- Education
- Lessons learned, including external case studies and internal testimonials

A sample communications framework is shown in Table 7.5. This framework assumes the presence of a TMO with program managers/project leads for each initiative. Each organization should modify the framework to fit its specific structure and needs.

Conclusion

The Value-Management Plan should evolve at various stages of the program, including planning, design, execution, and ongoing improvement so that the desired value identified during the Rapid ROI and Value Assessment is further defined and managed into reality. Chapter 8 provides a detailed explanation of the ROI analysis process and takes the telehealth example one step further.

Endnotes

1. "Telehealth's Potential to Transform Care Delivery | Kaiser Permanente." Business Health Care | Choose Better | Kaiser Permanente®. Accessed September 3, 2018. https://business.kaiserpermanente.org/insights/telehealths-potential-to-transform-care-delivery.
2. Ibid.
3. "Voice of the Customer." Wikipedia. August 23, 2018. https://en.wikipedia.org/wiki/Voice_of_the_customer.
4. Telehealth's Potential to Transform Care Delivery | Kaiser Permanente.
5. Gruessner, V. "The History of Remote Monitoring, Telemedicine Technology." MHealthIntelligence. November 6, 2015. https://mhealthintelligence.com/news/the-history-of-remote-monitoring-telemedicine-technology.
6. PricewaterhouseCoopers. "Virtual Health: Engaging Operational, Clinical and Technology Levers." PwC. Accessed September 8, 2018. https://www.pwc.com/us/en/healthcare/publications/virtual-health.html.
7. Ibid.
8. Fitchner, A. "Agile Vs. Lean: Yeah Yeah, What's the Difference?" The Hacker Chick Blog. February 5, 2017. https://hackerchick.com/agile-vs-lean-yeah-yeah-whats-the-difference/.

Chapter 8

Return on Investment Analysis: Building a Financial Model

Purpose

To provide a step-by-step outline for building a financial model for return on investment.

In this chapter, the reader will learn to

- Understand the three steps of a ROI analysis
- Identify and quantify capital, direct, and indirect operating costs
- Identify and quantify tangible and intangible benefits
- Understand four quantitative methods of calculating ROI
- Compare methods of ROI and the relative strengths and weaknesses of each

Understanding Return on Investment Analysis

Return on Investment (ROI) analysis is an important component of the Investment-Management Process discussed in Chapter 6 and part of the Value-Management Plan described in Chapter 7. Much like the adage "a square is a rectangle, but a rectangle is not a square," ROI is a form of value, but not all value takes the form of ROI. ROI is a financial metric—the percentage of dollars returned for a given investment/cost.[1] The breadth and depth of the analysis may vary depending on the complexity and scope of the program or project. Small projects may warrant only a simple cost-benefit analysis, whereas capital intensive multi-year efforts may require a robust, in-depth evaluation. ROI analysis consists of three key steps:

- *Step 1*: Identify and quantify costs.
- *Step 2*: Identify and quantify benefits.
- *Step 3*: Calculate ROI in a consistent manner.

The remaining sections of this chapter will address each step.

Step 1: Identify and Quantify Costs

While information technology vendors often provide estimates of the costs of hardware, software, and staffing, it is critically important to include the unique expenditures related to the individual organization, as well as the scope of change of the project or transformation program. In order to document the costs associated with the entire life of the project, costs should be divided into three categories:

- *Capital costs*: One-time costs associated with acquiring and implementing the HIT or transformation solution, including hardware and software, interfaces, outside consulting, any needed process redesign, implementation, and training. These costs are typically funded from the enterprise's capital budget. Table 8.1 provides a checklist of the typical types of capital-cost items and the source of cost estimates.
- *Operating expenses direct*: Ongoing operations costs associated with this solution, including license and maintenance fees, as well as human resources (FTEs).

Table 8.1   Capital Cost Checklist

Capital Cost Category	Typically Provided By		
	Vendor	Third Party Vendor	Internal
Hardware	✓		✓
Medical devices or communications systems		✓	
Packaged and customized software	✓		✓
Interfaces and integration	✓		✓
Network, peripherals, supplies, and equipment		✓	✓
Program development consulting		✓	
Process redesign		✓	
Initial data collection		✓	
Data conversion from legacy system	✓		✓
Archiving of legacy system data			✓
Facilities upgrades, including site preparation and renovation		✓	
End-user project management		✓	
Project planning, contract negotiation, and procurement		✓	✓
Project/program management	✓	✓	✓
Application development and deployment	✓		
Configuration management		✓	
Office accommodations, furniture, and related items		✓	
Initial user training	✓	✓	

(Continued)

Table 8.1 (Continued)   Capital Cost Checklist

	Typically Provided By		
Capital Cost Category	*Vendor*	*Third Party Vendor*	*Internal*
Workforce adjustment for affected employees		✓	
Transition costs, such as costs of running parallel systems or conversion of legacy systems		✓	
Quality assurance and post-implementation reviews	✓		✓

Oftentimes new initiatives require additional staff with skill sets not currently present in the enterprise. These costs will be incorporated into the organization's annual operating budgets over the life of the initiative.

■ *Operating expenses indirect*: Other associated peripheral costs incurred in support of the operation. These expenses may include activities such as help desk support, security, or administrative expenses.

Table 8.2 provides a checklist of the typical types of operating expenses associated with technology initiatives, where the expenses are incurred, and if they might be considered direct or indirect expenses.

While the checklists in Tables 8.1 and 8.2 are a starting point for cost identification, a full total cost of ownership will also consider the following:

■ Costs that arise due to specifics of the business and clinical operating environments. In the virtual visits example, considerations may include clinical, billing, telecommunications, education, and marketing support required to deliver the service.

■ Timing of costs. Some capital expenses may be spread over more than one year, and depending on how quickly

Table 8.2   Operating Cost Checklist

Operating Cost: Item	Direct		Indirect	
	User Department	IT	User Department	IT
Additional staffing (salaries and benefits)	✓	✓		
Software maintenance, subscriptions, and upgrades	✓			
Equipment leases	✓			
Facilities rental and utilities	✓			
Professional services	✓			
Ongoing training	✓	✓		
Reviews and audits	✓	✓	✓	
Data integrity			✓	✓
Security				✓
Privacy			✓	✓
Help desk				✓
Information technology policy management				✓

    an initiative is fully deployed, operating expenses may "ramp up" over several years.

■ Inflation, overhead, end-user support, and other costs as appropriate.

Table 8.3 provides an example of costs over a five-year period for the virtual visits initiative.

Step 2: Identify and Quantify Benefits

Tangible benefits are straightforward and relate directly to the bottom-line results of the ROI analysis. These benefits are concrete and represent measurable gains, such as increased

Table 8.3 Example—Identification and Quantification of Costs of Virtual Visits

Identification of Costs

1. Vendor estimates for hardware, software, implementation, and training

2. External consulting projections for process redesign and implementation

3. Internal costs for project staffing, training, and ongoing support

Quantification of Costs

Costs	Year 1	Year 2	Year 3	Year 4	Year 5	Notes
Hardware	$40,000	$0	—	—	—	Additional laptops with cameras
Software	$70,000	—	—	—	—	Initial software costs per vendor
Process redesign	$50,000	—	—	—	—	
Implementation/Training	$35,000	—	—	—	—	
Salaries	—	—	—	—	—	No additional IT staff. Provider costs included in benefits calculation

(Continued)

Table 8.3 (Continued) Example—Identification and Quantification of Costs of Virtual Visits

Quantification of Costs

Costs	Year 1	Year 2	Year 3	Year 4	Year 5	Notes
License/Maintenance	$60,000	$61,500	$63,038	$64,613	$66,229	Annual license fees with annual inflation of 2.5%
Depreciation	—	$39,000	$39,000	$39,000	$39,000	Depreciate software and hardware over 5 years
Total Costs	$255,000	$100,500	$102,038	$103,613	$105,229	

Notes: Ongoing costs include inflation factors. Depreciation starts in year 2 and is based on a 10-year schedule. Information technology will need to work with the finance department to determine which costs can be capitalized versus those that must be included in the operating budget. Finance will also be able to provide guidance as to the appropriate life of the investment for purposes of determining depreciation expenses.

revenues and cost reduction. Intangible benefits are less easily quantified yet can be measured. These measures can often tip the scale in favor of, or away from, a project when used as supporting documentation within the Value Realization Plan, as described in Chapter 7. Table 8.4 provides a framework for measuring tangible and intangible benefits, and Table 8.5 provides examples of tangible and intangible measures for virtual visits.

In the virtual visits example provided, non-urgent patients can be seen "on-demand" without waiting for appointment availability. A baseline, or current-state analysis, of third next available appointment indicates that primary care physicians are fully utilized. The Institute for Healthcare Improvement defines third next available appointment as the "average length of time in days between the day a patient makes a request for an appointment with a physician and the third available appointment for a new patient physical, routine exam, or return-visit exam. The third next available appointment is used rather than next available appointment since it is a more sensitive reflection of true appointment availability."[2] The desired outcome in offering virtual visits is to have advanced practice providers (APP) and physicians provide virtual visits and increase the volume of non-urgent visits per year. To calculate the dollar impact of the increase in visit volume, a number of variables must be analyzed to calculate the number of increased visits, the price, the blended cost of the practitioners conducting the visit, profit per visit, and the net cash flow over a multi-year period. Table 8.6 provides an example of the benefit calculation for the increased volume of visits through virtual visits.

Step 3: Calculate ROI in a Consistent Manner

Most healthcare organizations have established ROI thresholds and require ROI analysis as part of the approval process for enterprise-strategic-capital and operating expenditures. The

Table 8.4 Framework for Measuring Tangible and Intangible Benefits

Dimension	Benefit	Tangible				Quantifiable			
		Full	*Most*	*Some*	*Few*	*Full*	*Most*	*Some*	*Few*
Operational	Cost reduction	✓				✓			
	Revenue (cycle time reduction, charge capture, etc.)		✓			✓			
	Productivity improvement		✓			✓			
	Quality improvement			✓			✓		
	Customer-service improvement			✓			✓		
Managerial	Better resource management			✓			✓		
	Improved decision-making and planning			✓				✓	
	Performance improvement		✓				✓		

(Continued)

Table 8.4 (Continued) Framework for Measuring Tangible and Intangible Benefits

Dimension	Benefit	Tangible				Quantifiable			
		Full	Most	Some	Few	Full	Most	Some	Few
Strategic	Support market-share growth			✓		✓			
	Build capacity	✓				✓			
	Business innovation			✓				✓	
	Build cost leadership			✓				✓	
	Generate service differentiation			✓					✓
	Develop and expand partnerships				✓			✓	
IT infrastructure	Build flexibility for change				✓				✓
	IT cost reduction	✓				✓			
	Increased capability		✓				✓		
Organizational	Support organization change				✓				✓
	Facilitate learning				✓				✓
	Empowerment				✓				✓
	Build common vision and values				✓				✓

Table 8.5   Example—Identification and Quantification of Benefits for Virtual Visits

Name	Description	Type	Current State	Desired Outcome
Increase volume	Virtual visits allow non-urgent patients to be seen "on demand"	Tangible, tactical	PCPs are fully utilized with average third next available appointment	APPs and physicians provide virtual visits. Additional visits: • 365 year 1 • 1000 year 2 • 5000 year 3
Reduce costs	For at-risk populations, virtual visits cost less in terms of delivery costs as well as the use of lab, imaging, and pharmaceuticals	Tangible, strategic	Based on ABC Health historical claims, Typical primary care/urgent care visit paid claims are $650	Paid claims of $450/virtual visit
Increase capacity	Ability to have non-urgent patients seen outside of PCP office allows additional appointments to be "freed up"	Intangible, strategic	Many patients who cannot get an appointment go outside ABC Health System for care	Third next available appointment is less than two weeks
Improve patient satisfaction	Patients/consumers rate ABC Health in "top box" for the Patient Satisfaction survey	Intangible, strategic	CAHPS scores around "Getting Timely Care, Appointments, and Information" has only 50% in "Always" box	Top box score improvement to: • 70% in year 1 • 75% in year 2 • 80% in year 3

Table 8.6 Example—Benefit Calculation for Increased Volume of Non-Urgent Visits

Assumptions		
Description	*Value*	*Unit of Measure*
Time/visit	0.33	Hours
% Visits APP	55%	Percent
% Visits MD/DO	45%	Percent
Annual salary—APP	$125,000	Dollars
Annual salary—MD/DO	$250,000	Dollars
Benefits	30%	Percent
Average hourly rate, including benefits APP	$78.13	Dollars
Average hourly rate, including benefits MD/DO	$156.25	Dollars
Annual inflation rate, labor costs	3.0%	Percent

Item	Year 1	Year 2	Year 3	Year 4	Year 5
Average number of visits/day	1	8	15	30	50
Number of visits/year	365	2,920	5,475	10,950	18,250
Price per visit	$50.00	$50.00	$55.00	$55.00	$60.00
Variable cost/visit	$37.76	$38.89	$40.06	$41.26	$42.50
Profit/visit	$12.24	$11.11	$14.94	$13.74	$17.50
Net cash flow	$4,467	$32,432	$81,796	$150,433	$319,381

exact method or combination of methods will depend on the preferences of the board and senior management and should be defined in the Investment-Management Process. The method used is not as important as the consistent application of the methodology across all investment categories including joint ventures, service lines, information technology, etc. Traditional ROI analyses are relatively straightforward and typically consist of building a financial model, usually in a spreadsheet format.

Cash Flow Analysis: The Foundation

Cash flow analysis is the first step and is used as the foundation for all calculations as seen in Figure 8.1. Cash flow demonstrates the total benefits (additional revenues or costs reduced), less total expenses over a specific period. Cash flows may be negative during the first year or years of a project due to capital outlays and minimal benefits and grow increasingly positive as benefits are realized. Another important calculation is the cumulative cash flow, that is, the sum of all cash flows from the start of the project to a given point in time. The cumulative cash flow at year three, for example, would be the sum of the cash flows for years one, two, and three. As illustrated in the virtual visits example in Figure 8.1, cash flow is negative for years one through three and becomes positive in year four.

In addition to the foundational cash flow analysis, there are a number of financial measures available to identify ROI. Four key measurement methods are explained in this chapter:

- Payback (breakeven) period
- Benefit-cost ratio
- Net present value (NPV)
- Internal rate of return (IRR)

		ABC Health System Return on Investment Analysis 8/27/2018					
		Year 1	Year 2	Year 3	Year 4	Year 5	Year 6
Total Benefits	$	-	$ 35,402	$ 227,079	$ 382,593	$ 492,577	$ 684,381
Total Costs	$	255,000	$ 100,500	$ 102,038	$ 103,613	$ 105,229	$ 106,884
Cash Flow	$	(255,000)	$ (65,098)	$ 125,042	$ 278,979	$ 387,349	$ 577,496
Cumulative Cash Flow		(255,000)	(320,098)	(195,056)	83,924	471,272	1,048,768

Figure 8.1 Cash flow example—virtual visits.

For each, we provide the general formula, list strengths and weaknesses, and show the Excel spreadsheet equivalent, including formula.

Payback Period or Breakeven Analysis

The payback or breakeven period is the length of time needed to recover a project's initial cost, not taking into account the time value of money. The calculation for payback period is defined in Figure 8.2.

In the virtual visits example, the last year with a negative cumulative cash flow from the foundational cash flow is year 3. The cumulative cash flow for Last Year with Negative Cumulative

$$PP = A + \frac{-B}{C}$$

Where:

A = Last Year with a Negative Cumulative Cash Flow
B = Cumulative Cash flow for Last Year with Negative Cumulative Cash Flow
C = Cash Flow for the Year (Only) in the First year with a Positive Cash Flow

In this case, $$PP = 3 + \frac{-(195,056)}{278,979}$$

Strengths:
- Easy to understand for non-financial managers

Weaknesses:
- Not as financially precise as other measures of financial return
- Tends to produce a bias toward projects with early returns, rather than measuring the magnitude of the return

ABC Health System
Return on Investment Analysis
8/27/2018

	Year	Year 1	Year 2	Year 3	Year 4	Year 5	Year 6
		1	2	3	4	5	6
Total Benefits		$ -	$ 35,402	$ 227,079	$ 382,593	$ 492,577	$ 684,381
Total Costs		$ 255,000	$ 100,500	$ 102,038	$ 103,613	$ 105,229	$ 106,884
Cash Flow		$ (255,000)	$ (65,098)	$ 125,042	$ 278,979	$ 387,349	$ 577,496
Cumulative Cash Flow		(255,000)	(320,098)	(195,056)	83,924	471,272	1,048,768
Payback Period Formula		=IF(C13<0,IF(D13<0,IF(E13<0,IF(F13<0,IF(G13<0,IF(H13<0,"Greater than 6 years", 5+(-G13/H12)),4+(-F13/G12)),3+(-E13/F12)),2+(-D13/E12)),1+(-C13/D12)),"Less than 1 year")					
Payback Period		3.70 Years					

Figure 8.2 Payback period or breakeven calculation.

Cash Flow is ($195,056), and the Cash Flow for the Year (only) in the First year with a Positive Cumulative Cash Flow is $278,979, so the Payback Period is 3.7 years. Most organizations have defined payback period timeframes for acceptance.

Benefit-Cost Ratio

The benefit-cost ratio calculates total benefits over the life of the project compared to the total costs over the life of the project. In our virtual visits example, the total benefits for years 1–6 are $1,822,033, and the total costs are $773,264. As illustrated in Figure 8.3, the Benefit-Cost Ratio is calculated to be 2.36.

A benefit-cost ratio of 1.0 would indicate that the benefits would equal the costs exactly. Thus, the "go/no-go" hurdle would be to have a benefit-cost ratio greater than 1.0 and would depend on the organization's current direction as to the exact minimum acceptable ratio.

Net Present Value

Net present value (NPV) is a measure that accounts for the "time value of money." That is, the NPV compares the proposed investment with the cost associated with funding the investment (e.g., raising funds through bond issuances or investing in other financial market venues that yield a certain annual percentage rate). Another way to think of it is, "If I invested money in a fund at x% (my minimum expected return), would I be better off than investing in this project?" Net present value is calculated by summing the net cash flows over the life of the project and adjusting for the cost of capital or minimum acceptable rate of return (MARR). The NPV can be calculated for every period during the life of the project. The calculation for NPV, assuming a hurdle rate (or MARR) of 3%, is illustrated in Figure 8.4.

The key to this analysis is to correctly and completely identify costs and benefits and their associated timing. Typically, one should expect a positive NPV at project end for

$$BC = \frac{\sum_{n=0}^{N} B_n}{\sum_{n=0}^{N} (Cn + On)}$$

Where:

n = the time period (typically a year)

N = the total number of time periods

B = total benefits for a specific time period

C = Capital invested in a specific time period

O = Operating expenses in a specific time period

Strengths:
- Simple to calculate and easy to understand

Weaknesses:
- Does not account for the magnitude of the benefit

ABC Health System
Return on Investment Analysis
8/27/2018

	Year	Year 1 1	Year 2 2	Year 3 3	Year 4 4	Year 5 5	Year 6 6
Total Benefits		$ -	$ 35,402	$ 227,079	$ 382,593	$ 492,577	$ 684,381
Total Costs		$ 255,000	$ 100,500	$ 102,038	$ 103,613	$ 105,229	$ 106,884
Cash Flow		$ (255,000)	$ (65,098)	$ 125,042	$ 278,979	$ 387,349	$ 577,496
Cumulative Cash Flow		(255,000)	(320,098)	(195,056)	83,924	471,272	1,048,768
Total Costs Years 1-6		$ 773,264					
Total Benefits Years 1-6		$ 1,822,033					
Benefit Cost Ratio		2.36					
Benefit Cost Ratio Formula		=SUM(C9:H9)/SUM(C10:H10)					

Figure 8.3   Benefit-cost ratio calculation.

it to be considered a "go" for implementation. This calculation (similar to payback period and benefit-cost ratio) is an initial phase gate through which proposed initiatives must pass.

Internal Rate of Return

The internal rate of return (IRR) is a companion calculation to NPV and shows what returns on an investment can be

$$NPV(i) = \sum_{n=0}^{N} \frac{F_n}{(1+i)^n}$$

Where:

i = cost of cash/hurdle rate (opportunity interest rate or MARR)
n = The time period (typically a year)
N = total number of time periods
F = net cash flow for a specific period

Strengths:
- A straightforward, precise, calculation of the expected financial value of a proposed investment

Weaknesses:
- May be difficult for non-financially oriented managers to understand

	ABC Health System Return on Investment Analysis 8/27/2018						
		Year 1	Year 2	Year 3	Year 4	Year 5	Year 6
	Year	1	2	3	4	5	6
Total Benefits		$ -	$ 35,402	$ 227,079	$ 382,593	$ 492,577	$ 684,381
Total Costs		$ 255,000	$ 100,500	$ 102,038	$ 103,613	$ 105,229	$ 106,884
Cash Flow		$ (255,000)	$ (65,098)	$ 125,042	$ 278,979	$ 387,349	$ 577,496
Cumulative Cash Flow		(255,000)	(320,098)	(195,056)	83,924	471,272	1,048,768
Net Present Value		$ (247,573)	$ (308,934)	$ (194,503)	$ 53,367	$ 387,497	$ 871,141
Assumptions:							
NPV Rate		3.00%					
Net Present Value Formula		=NPV(C18,$C12:H12)					

Figure 8.4 Net present value calculation.

expected as a percentage of the investment. Here, the "go/no-go" hurdle is tied to the current prevailing interest rate for investments. For example, if the enterprise can earn 10% through an arbitrage process for their cash reserves and an investment will only yield 5%, it may not make sense to make the IT investment. There are a number of ways to calculate IRR. Most spreadsheets can automatically perform this function, but if done manually, a formula is shown in Figure 8.5.

The calculation requires an initial guess at the interest rate. Typically, organizations start with their specified

$$0 = P_0 + P_1/(1+IRR) + P_2/(1+IRR)^2 + P_3/(1+IRR)^3 + \ldots + P_n/(1+IRR)^n$$

Where

$P_0, P_1, \ldots P_n$ = the cash flows in periods 1, 2, ... n, respectively

IRR = the project's internal rate of return.

Strengths:
- Calculates the return on the original money invested

Weaknesses:
- At times, it can give you conflicting answers when compared to NPV for mutually exclusive project

ABC Health System
Return on Investment Analysis
8/27/2018

	Year	Year 1 1	Year 2 2	Year 3 3	Year 4 4	Year 5 5	Year 6 6
Total Benefits		$ -	$ 35,402	$ 227,079	$ 382,593	$ 492,577	$ 684,381
Total Costs		$ 255,000	$ 100,500	$ 102,038	$ 103,613	$ 105,229	$ 106,884
Cash Flow		$ (255,000)	$ (65,098)	$ 125,042	$ 278,979	$ 387,349	$ 577,496
Cumulative Cash Flow		(255,000)	(320,098)	(195,056)	83,924	471,272	1,048,768
Internal Rate of Return			#NUM!	-42%	10%	34%	49%
Assumptions:							
IRR Capital Hurdle Rate		5.00%					
Internal Rate of Return Formula		=IRR(SC12:H12,C18)					

Figure 8.5 Internal rate of return calculation.

"hurdle rate" (5% in the virtual visits example). In general, the IRR value cannot be derived analytically unless using calculus. Instead, IRR must be found by using trial and error to determine the appropriate rate. Additionally, changes in the economy must be considered so that any anticipated major upward or downward fluctuations are included in evaluating the project's return vis-á-vis the prevailing economy. In addition to the manual calculation formula, Figure 8.5 provides the IRR results from the virtual visits initiative. The spreadsheet notation "#NUM" indicates IRR cannot be calculated for years one and two in the virtual visits initiative since there is no return in those years.

In summary, there are multiple methods for calculating ROI. Each approach tells a different story, and it is important to understand the relative strengths and weaknesses of each. Measures are complementary and are intended to guide, rather than serve as a substitute for decision-making. None of the measures account for intangible or qualitative metrics. Organizations can combine these measures in a format such as the Management Overview as shown in Figure 8.6. This Management Overview allows Senior Leadership to review all aspects of the financial impact in a one-page format.

Conclusion

This chapter has provided the details behind the calculations presented in the Investment-Management Process and Value-Realization Plan. A number of considerations play into the development of capital and operating costs, as well as in the identification of the various levels of benefits, both tangible and intangible. Various ROI methodologies provide differing insight and can complement each other when comparing and managing the projects/programs within the overall portfolio. Ultimately, each organization must decide how to consistently apply measures of ROI across investments to best create its capital investment portfolio.

ABC Health System
ROI Management Overview

	Year 1	Year 2	Year 3	Year 4	Year 5	Year 6
Benefits	$ -	$ 35,402	$ 227,079	$ 382,593	$ 492,577	$ 684,381
Total Expenses	255,000	100,500	102,038	103,613	105,229	106,884
Cash Flow	$ (255,000)	$ (65,098)	$ 125,042	$ 278,979	$ 387,349	$ 577,496
Cumulative Cash Flow	$ (255,000)	$ (320,098)	$ (195,056)	$ 83,924	$ 471,272	$ 1,048,768
Net Present Value	$ (247,573)	$ (308,934)	$ (194,503)	$ 53,367	$ 387,497	$ 871,141
Internal Rate of Return			-42%	10%	34%	49%

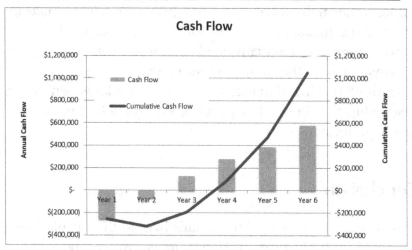

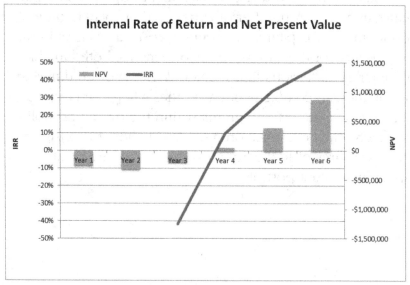

Figure 8.6 Management overview.

Endnotes

1. "The Difference Between Value and ROI." The Difference
   Between Value and ROI |. June 12, 2009. Accessed
   September 14, 2018. https://metricsman.wordpress.
   com/2009/06/12/the-difference-between-value-and-roi/.
2. "Third Next Available Appointment." Institute for Healthcare
   Improvement. Accessed September 14, 2018. http://www.ihi.org/
   resources/Pages/Measures/ThirdNextAvailableAppointment.aspx.

Chapter 9

Making Value Actionable: The Role of the Transformation Scorecard Process

Purpose

To focus on transformation portfolio performance measurement and make value actionable.

In this chapter, the reader will review

- The basic concepts of Balanced Scorecards
- How to adapt the Balanced Scorecard to the Transformation Portfolio
- The Transformation Scorecard Process, including cascading scorecards for strategic initiatives, programs, and projects
- Success criteria for the Transformation Scorecard Process

Adapting the Balanced Scorecard

In their groundbreaking work *The Balanced Scorecard*, Kaplan and Norton developed a management system for measuring organizational performance in four areas: financial, internal business processes, learning and growth, and customer relationships.[1] Prior to that time, the primary performance measurement system for business had a financial focus. This "Balanced Scorecard" approach, as shown in Figure 9.1, was adapted and used by senior leaders in healthcare, as well as other industries such as banking, energy, and retail. The scorecard's four components are supported by a delineation of the specific objectives, corresponding metrics, targets (internal or external benchmarks), and specific initiatives that must be carried out to accomplish the objectives. The balanced scorecard provides a comprehensive framework for translating an organization's vision and strategies into coherent performance measures and actions for entities, departments, divisions, and individual contributors across the enterprise. In an ideal world, everyone from the board to the front line would understand how leaders and their teams support the big picture.

Healthcare executives often use the terms scorecard and dashboard interchangeably. For the purposes of this book, the two are defined as follows:

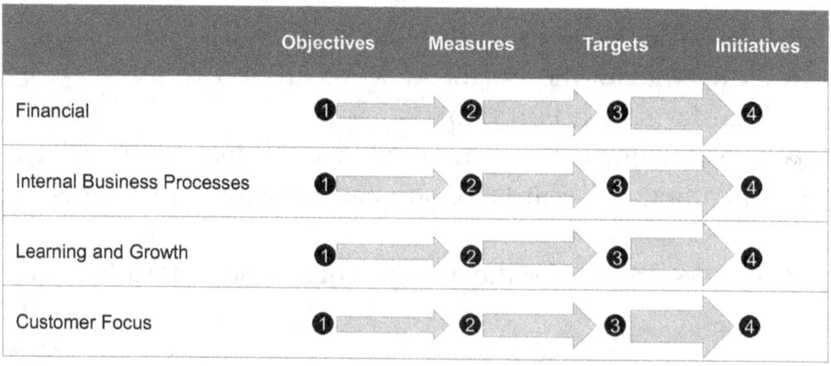

	Objectives	Measures	Targets	Initiatives
Financial	①	②	③	④
Internal Business Processes	①	②	③	④
Learning and Growth	①	②	③	④
Customer Focus	①	②	③	④

Figure 9.1   Balanced scorecard measurement system.

- *Scorecards*: Measure and compare performance against desired goals and outcomes. Scorecards evaluate the success and failure of key initiatives based on key performance indicators (KPIs) established at the beginning of the initiative, as defined within key programs and their projects. Scorecards provide a high-level overview of a health system's strategic improvement goals (e.g., reduce readmissions, increase average patient satisfaction, and reduce average or turnaround times). Scorecards are long-term and slow to change as goals change over weeks, months, or years. They leverage information from multiple source systems, such as enterprise data warehouses, which combine EHR, financial, and patient satisfaction data with external data such as benchmarks to track strategic goals.[2]
- *Dashboards*: Provide real-time or near real-time operational information encompassing tactical scenarios. Dashboards are more detailed and tell operational leaders what's happening now using interactive metrics with drill-down capabilities. They enable comparison of current and historical healthcare data and allow for daily, constant monitoring of KPIs and other data.[3]

As healthcare leaders develop strategies to support population health management and the transition to value, many cite the use of dashboarding and scorecards as effective ways to measure performance. Metrics focusing on the performance of specific strategies, programs, and projects, when compared to desired norms, targets, or goals, are an essential component of driving transformational change. As healthcare organizations transition from volume to value, the balanced scorecard can be adapted to focus on transformation.

The Transformation Scorecard Process

The Transformation Scorecard Process is a summary of the current status of a single transformation initiative and is

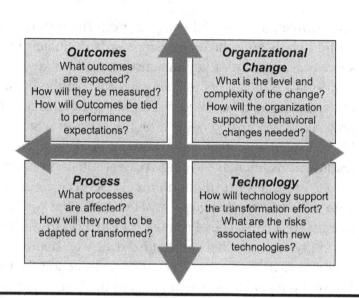

Figure 9.2   Dimensions of the transformation scorecard.

an important means of communicating and documenting transformation progress, issues, and status to key stakeholders across various levels of the organization. Just as a balanced scorecard has four dimensions of measurement, the transformation scorecard measures performance in the dimensions of outcomes, organizational change, process, and technology, as illustrated in Figure 9.2.

The objectives of a robust Transformation Scorecard Process include

- Defining transformation initiative goals, objectives, timelines, accountabilities, and interdependencies
- Linking the transformation initiative to organizational strategic objectives
- Developing consistent, comprehensive reporting for proactive transformation program management and early intervention when appropriate
- Implementing comprehensive, structured communications focusing on transformation stakeholders

- Providing input for the prioritization of programs, projects, and resources
- Maintaining an issue-tracking system and managing an issue-resolution process for all transformation projects
- Ensuring understanding and communicating accomplishments across all levels of the transformation initiative

Ideally, the Value-Management Plan will be aligned with the Transformation Scorecard Process, and key ROI and value metrics will be tracked throughout the entire life cycle of the initiative. When the Transformation Scorecard Process is fully functional, the organization as a whole, including senior management, will realize the benefits that are outlined in Table 9.1.

Table 9.1   Benefits of the Transformation Scorecard Process

Benefits to the Organization	*Benefits to Senior Leadership*
Increased awareness of all transformation initiatives being planned or underway	Comprehensive overview of transformation initiatives
Understanding of the linkages and dependencies between initiatives	Demonstrated linkage of initiatives with strategic goals of organization
Improved communication within and between initiative teams	Clear understanding of initiative objectives, activities, and resource requirements
Improved scheduling of projects, activities, and resources	Accurate and timely information of initiative progress
Enhanced awareness of opportunities to participate in transforming the organization	Standardized project planning, tracking, and reporting
Focused implementation of change initiatives	Comprehensive overview of all initiative issues

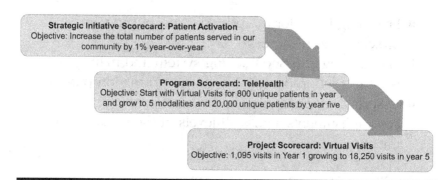

Figure 9.3 Cascading measures.

The Transformation Scorecard Process consists of three levels of cascading reports, including the Strategic Initiative, Program, and Project Scorecards. Desired value can be translated into objectives, measures, and targets. By cascading or linking the three scorecards, stakeholders can understand the cause-and-effect relationships of the key performance indicators across the entire transformation portfolio. Figure 9.3 illustrates the desired value of one objective within the Patient Activation Strategic Initiative and a cascaded objective, measure, and target for the Telehealth Program and Virtual Visits Project.

The Transformation Scorecard Process enables portfolio-wide status briefings and should follow a structured and timely process for developing and submitting each report to the appropriate decision-making group. Figure 9.4 illustrates and summarizes the reporting process for the cascading

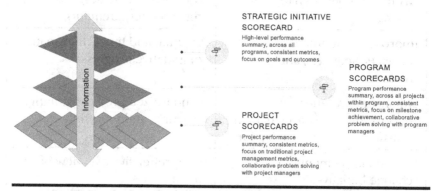

Figure 9.4 Transformation scorecard reporting process.

reports—The Strategic Initiative, Program, and Project Scorecards.

Each scorecard, and the reporting process that fulfills the distinct purpose of each scorecard for use by different individuals and groups, is described below:

■ *Strategic initiative scorecard*: The current state of each transformation initiative or strategy within the transformation portfolio is summarized and all programs within the strategic initiative are rolled up in this report. Typically, the Transformation Management Office would be responsible for tracking and reporting on the status of the strategic initiative to governance and other team members. The scorecard is deliverables-based and focuses on the organization's achievement of goals and outcomes. This scorecard, reported at a frequency determined by governance, should present very high-level information, only raising high priority issues or accomplishments. Strategic Initiative Scorecards allow the board, transformation governance, and executive management to be continually apprised of the status and changes occurring in all current strategies. The reporting process helps management track progress, resource utilization, and achievement of outcomes/ goals, which may include quantitative ROI or qualitative values. The Patient Activation Strategy addressed in previous chapters is an example of an enterprise initiative which might benefit from a Strategic Initiative Scorecard. Figure 9.5 illustrates the overall progress, specific outcomes against targets, and the separate programs of the initiative for the example Patient Activation initiative.

■ *Program scorecard*: The Program Manager uses the Program Scorecard to report all projects within a program in summary form. The Program Scorecard describes the high-level status of each project within a program and supports the communication of key accomplishments as well as planned activities. Additionally, the report allows

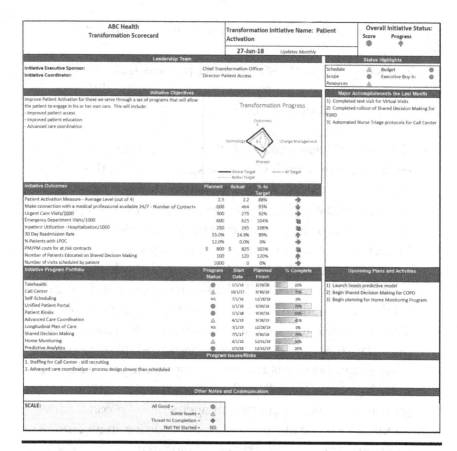

ABC Health Transformation Scorecard		Transformation Initiative Name: Patient Activation		Overall Initiative Status:	
		27-Jun-18 *Updates Monthly*		Score Progress ● ↑	

Leadership Team		**Status Highlights**	
Initiative Executive Sponsor:	Chief Transformation Officer	Schedule ⚠	Budget ●
Initiative Coordinator:	Director Patient Access	Scope ●	Executive Buy-In ●
		Resources ⚠	

Initiative Objectives

Improve Patient Activation for those we serve through a set of programs that will allow the patient to engage in his or her own care. This will include:
- Improved patient access
- Improved patient education
- Advanced care coordination

Transformation Progress

Major Accomplishments the Last Month
1) Completed test visit for Virtual Visits
2) Completed rollout of Shared Decision Making for ESRD
3) Automated Nurse Triage protocols for Call Center

Initiative Outcomes	Planned	Actual	% to Target	
Patient Activation Measure - Average Level (out of 4)	2.5	2.2	88%	→
Make connection with a medical professional available 24/7 - Number of Contacts	500	464	93%	↓
Urgent Care Visits/1000	300	275	92%	→
Emergency Department Visits/1000	600	625	104%	↘
Inpatient Utilization - Hospitalization/1000	250	265	106%	↘
30 Day Readmission Rate	15.0%	14.9%	99%	↑
% Patients with LPOC	12.0%	0.0%	0%	→
PM/PM costs for at risk contracts	$ 800	$ 825	103%	↘
Number of Patients Educated on Shared Decision Making	100	120	120%	↑
Number of visits scheduled by patient	1000	0	0%	→

Initiative Program Portfolio	Program Status	Start Date	Planned Finish	% Complete		Upcoming Plans and Activities
Telehealth	●	1/1/18	3/29/20	25%		1) Launch Sepsis predictive model
Call Center	⚠	10/1/17	9/30/18	75%		2) Begin Shared Decision Making for COPD
Self-Scheduling	NS	7/1/18	12/28/18	0%		3) Begin planning for Home Monitoring Program
Unified Patient Portal	●	1/1/18	9/30/18	75%		
Patient Kiosks	●	1/1/18	9/30/16	95%		
Advanced Care Coordination	⚠	4/1/19	9/28/19	45%		
Longitudinal Plan of Care	NS	7/1/19	12/28/19	0%		
Shared Decision Making	●	7/1/17	9/30/18	75%		
Home Monitoring	⚠	4/1/18	12/31/18	50%		
Predictive Analytics	●	2/1/18	12/31/19	25%		

Program Issues/Risks

1. Staffing for Call Center - still recruiting
2. Advanced care coordination - process design slower than scheduled

Other Notes and Communication

SCALE:		
	All Good =	●
	Some Issues =	⚠
	Threat to Completion =	◆
	Not Yet Started =	NS

Figure 9.5 Strategic initiative scorecard—patient activation example.

key stakeholders to know the status of all projects related to a program, as well as the inter-project issues, dependencies, timelines, value lever relationships, etc. The Telehealth Program described in Chapter 7 should be tracked using a Program Scorecard and is shown in Figure 9.6.

■ *Project scorecard*: The Project Scorecard, used by the project team and the project manager to report individual project progress to program management, is activity based and in summary form. Its purpose is to identify new, persisting, and resolved issues, not to list all performed and anticipated activities. Detailed scorecards encourage project managers to reflect on the current state of the project. Through reporting, project managers can account for key

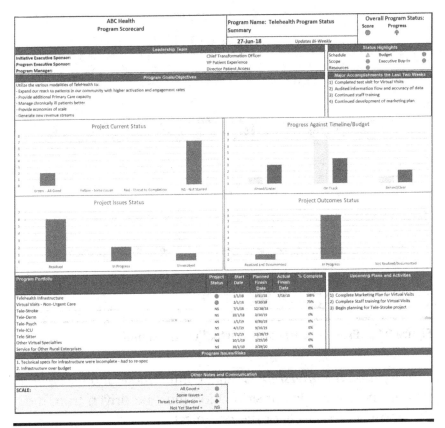

Figure 9.6   Program scorecard—telehealth example.

events and be proactive in setting goals and addressing issues. A Virtual Visits project example, as discussed in Chapter 8 and depicted in Figure 9.7, provides granular detail on specific milestones, and the degree of completion for planned activities as well as project-specific risks.

Critical Success Factors for Use of the Transformation Scorecard

Several factors influence the overall success of the Transformation Scorecard Process as well as the overall transformation portfolio, including

ABC Health
Project Scorecard

Project Name: Virtual Visits
Program Name: TeleHealth

27-Jun-18 *Updates Weekly*

Overall Initiative Status:
Score ● Progress ↑

Leadership Team

Program Executive Sponsor:	VP Patient Experience
Program Manager:	Director, Patient Access Center
Project Manager:	PMO Project Manager

Status Highlights

Schedule	●	Budget	▲
Scope	▲	Executive Buy-In	●
Resources	●		

Project Goals/Objectives

Pilot the use of TeleHealth services by providing non-urgent care access (e.g. sore throat, pink-eye) through our patient portal to enrolled patients. This will require additional infrastructure (video) to tie to our current EHR

Major Accomplishments Last Week

1) Worked with marketing department to identify target audiences, messaging and channels

Key Milestones / Deliverables	Task Status	Start Date	Planned Finish Date	Actual Finish Date	% Complete
Form and kick off the Project Steering Team and Working Groups	●	2/1/18	2/9/18	2/5/18	100%
Workflow Design	●	2/12/18	3/16/18	3/23/18	100%
Configure Flow Sheets	●	3/23/18	4/20/18	4/20/18	100%
Test Workflows	●	4/20/18	5/25/18	5/31/18	100%
Identify Staff	●	3/15/18	3/29/18	3/29/18	100%
Perform Test Visit	●	5/14/18	6/8/18	6/12/18	100%
Audit Information Flow	●	6/8/18	6/15/18	6/15/18	100%
Develop Marketing Plan	▲	6/18/18	6/29/18		75%
Train Staff	●	6/18/18	7/16/18		25%
Launch Marketing	NS	9/16/18	9/30/18		
Go-Live	NS	9/30/18	10/7/18		

Upcoming Plans and Activities

1) Complete Marketing Plan and get Steering Team approval
2) Continue training

Project Issues/Risks

Other Notes and Communication

SCALE:
All Good = ●
Some Issues = ▲
Threat to Completion = ◆
Not Yet Started = NS

Figure 9.7 Project scorecard—virtual visits example.

- *Top-down leadership*: C-Suite commitment and ownership are necessary as transformation must be driven from the most senior levels of the organization.
- *Consistent application*: Whatever form the scorecard takes, it must be used in the same manner across all transformation initiatives. All stakeholders need to agree on the measures being tracked, as well as the definition of success.
- *Accountability*: For each measure, a key point person should be assigned responsibility for managing the activities and processes that are being measured.
- *Collaborative solution development*: Cross-functional relationships need to exist, facilitating productive discussion and real-time problem solving to develop solutions that are cross-cutting and multidisciplinary.
- *Team participation*: Although top-down support of performance measurement is essential for the organization, the value of team participation at the

frontline level cannot be stressed enough. The value of the investment is maximized, and practical approaches to process improvement are realized, by involving the people who are actually affected by the change.

■ *Nonpunitive forum for problem resolution*: The very nature of transformation through technology initiatives dictates that changes in plans and processes must occur as part of the transformation effort. A safe, nonthreatening, real-time venue in which to resolve issues is key to making the transformation a success.

■ *Techniques and tools*: Scorecards must be visually intuitive and easy to understand. Avoid IT/technology-specific language. Clearly identify what is being measured and define specific time periods. Ensure the scorecard contains the most recently available performance data, but be sure to track key performance indicators over time. Continue to measure progress in all four areas to ensure balance. If the scorecard is paper-based, it should be formatted with summary information on a single sheet. More detailed information (preferably a single sheet for each quadrant) can be attached as appropriate. If a web-based reporting system is being used, utilize hot links to allow the viewer to drill down to additional detail. The layers should go from general to specific and may even include raw data.

The most important critical success factor, however, is based on educating all stakeholders regarding interpretation of the cascading reports. Essential elements of sound Transformation Scorecard messaging should consider

■ Messaging designed to meet the needs of specific audiences, communicate in non-technical terms, include common definitions, address how metrics were identified, and explain how calculations are made.

■ Risks, problems or issues, and mitigation plans must be articulated so that all involved understand the actions that must be taken based on the importance of certain metrics and the metric's role in value realization and creation.

■ Period updates that consider the evolution of the transformation portfolio. Specific plans for improvement, redesign, or innovation must be communicated as part of the scorecard package.

Conclusion

The Transformation Scorecard Process should be the primary measurement mechanism across the organization's transformation portfolio, but no two organization's score process will look alike. Consistency, communication, measurement, and alignment with enterprise transformation is critical. The next and final chapter of this book addresses the most important aspect of transformation and innovation— changing the way we change.

Endnotes

1. Kaplan, R. S. and D. P. Norton. "The Balanced Scorecard – Measures That Drive Performance." *Harvard Business Review.* 1992.
2. "Healthcare Dashboards vs. Scorecards to Improve Outcomes." Health Catalyst. September 6, 2018. https://www.healthcatalyst. com/healthcare-dashboards-vs-scorecards-to-improve-outcomes.
3. Ibid.

Chapter 10

Transformation and Population Health: Changing the Way Healthcare Changes

Purpose

To introduce the concept of changing the way healthcare changes through transformation and population-health management.

In this chapter, the reader will review

- Kotter's original Change Management Model and an update
- The difference in change management and transformational change
- New strategic imperatives for population health
- Technology enabled population segments
- A conclusion and an introduction to the next book in the series

Transformational Change and Population Health

Change management has always been a key to successful HIT implementation. Defined as "the human side of electronic medical records implementations (EMRs), the human-focused work of engaging and preparing people to succeed in the new world of EMRs,"[1] this type of change focused on automation and represented incremental improvement within existing healthcare organizations, processes, and operating models. Change management activities applied to individuals, groups, and the whole organization, and involved stakeholder communications, training, team building, issue management, workflow design, meeting, and project management. If change management was not a priority during the EHR implementation, problems such as limited understanding of the case for EHRs, workarounds, too much customization, added cost, and of course limited return on investment and value realization were the results. For many, following a methodology, such as Kotter's Change Model, provided step by step actions for preparing the organization for change, engaging stakeholders, and delivering quick wins and long-term sustainable results (Figure 10.1).

The Office of the National Coordinator for Healthcare Information Technology encouraged the use of Kotter's

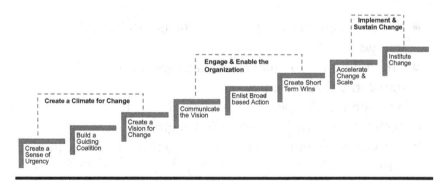

Figure 10.1   Kotter's change model.[2]

model in their 2016 primer, *Change Management in EHR Implementation*.[3] Originally designed in 1996, Kotter recognized that the pace of change had increased since he launched the influential model and updated these concepts in 2014 in his book *Accelerate.* In summary, the newer book still follows the original model and suggests

- Run the steps concurrently and continuously
- Form a large volunteer army from up, down, and across the organization to serve as the change engine
- Function in a network flexibly and agilely outside of, but in conjunction with, a traditional hierarchy
- Operate as if strategy is a dynamic force by constantly seeking opportunities, identifying initiatives to capitalize on them, and completing them quickly and efficiently[4]

From a semantic perspective, many confuse change management with transformational change. Transformational change is the least understood and most complex type of change facing healthcare organizations today. Rather than focusing on a finite initiative with well-defined shifts, transformation provides a portfolio of change, often with intersecting and interdependent programs and projects.[5] A radical shift from one state of being to another, transformational change is largely uncertain at the beginning and emerges in a new state as a product of the change process itself.[6]

The transition from Stage, 1.0 Brick-and-Mortar Healthcare, to Stage 3.0, Digital Health and Connected Care, explored in Chapter 2, describes the profound combination of market trends, competitive forces, differentiating capabilities, and a variety of emerging technologies that will drive transformational change for each organization. Strategic imperatives are different for each organization and dependent on progress toward clinical integration and value-based contractual arrangements with payers. Enterprise priorities often include

- *Margin management*: Maximizing revenue growth and streamlining cost per case.
- *Market expansion*: Extending service lines beyond existing capacities and capabilities.
- *Access enhancement*: Leveraging existing and creating new access points to acquire and retain patients.
- *Network keepage*: Improving referral management processes for attributed patients and improving deployment of specialist and primary-care resources.
- *Throughput management*: Ensuring efficient and effective care transitions.
- *Consumer relationship management*: Enhancing patient and consumer engagement and activation.
- *Insight-driven decision-making*: Integrating data from a variety of internal and external sources to drive decision making across the continuum of care.
- *Business model innovation*: Using new combinations of data, technology, and operating models to create new sources of revenue, cost efficiencies, and customer self-management or satisfaction levels.

While digital tools, analytics, and new care management platforms are essential to drive the strategic imperatives mentioned above, the challenges will not be technological. In his *Harvard Business Review* article, "Why Transformation Efforts Fail," Kotter suggests that transformational change sticks when it "becomes the way we do things around here. Change must be institutionalized into the corporate culture."[7] Yet, humans have a natural tendency to resist change and leaders often struggle to:

- Collaborate and apply team-based, network decision-making methods alongside hierarchical, command, and control organization structures

- Involve front-line clinicians, care providers, affiliates, and partners in planning change to work practices, processes, and operating models
- Learn from insights derived from descriptive, diagnostic, predictive, and prescriptive analytics rather than jumping to solutions based on past experience or making consensus-based decisions
- Use a systematic, holistic approach to change versus addressing symptoms of a problem
- Move the needle across key measures rather than focusing on compliance and reporting of outcomes and indicators

To transform the healthcare enterprise, leaders will have to manage change in new and different ways and ultimately change the way healthcare changes. Connected health services are expected to dramatically transform clinician-to-clinician, provider-to-patient, and consumer-driven interactions via technology-enabled consultation, direct patient care, self-management, and educational services. Electronic intensive care, emergency, specialty, urgent, and primary care are joining remote monitoring and hospital at home as transformative services. A wide array of mobile apps, social media, online support groups, scheduling tools, patient portals, and other technology-based innovations are having dramatic impact on the healthcare industry's ability to create new forms of value. Figure 10.2 illustrates key population segments and the technologies that may disrupt care delivery and business models in the future.

In the book *Rethinking Return on Investment: The Challenge of Population Health Management*, the subject of changing the way healthcare changes will be explored in more detail. Specific implications for investment, the potential returns in improved outcomes, reduced cost of care, and an enhanced consumer experience will be addressed. In order to ultimately drive value, new capabilities and ways of thinking

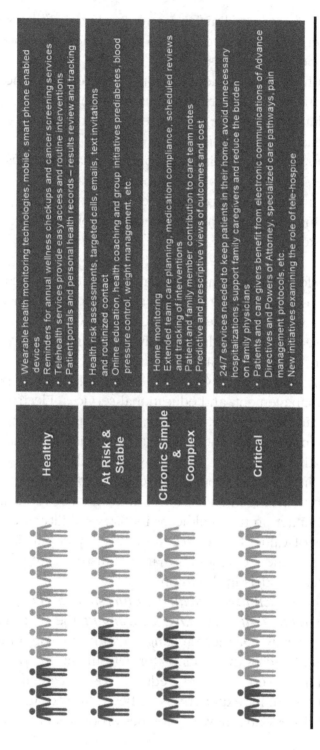

Figure 10.2 Population segments and technology use cases.

about the way we work will be needed. While uncertainty will remain, healthcare delivery systems will have to challenge their existing paradigms and deliver value-based care through digital transformation and innovations. The next book in this series will cover topics such as

- Care models for high-risk and rising-risk patients
- Experimentation versus scaling
- The changing role of informatics, analytics, quality, and information technology
- Rethinking the siloes, consumer centric design, and operations
- New decision-making and operating models

Conclusion

Ultimately, the ROI and value of healthcare information technology are not about the tools, systems, applications, or infrastructure, they are about change. As defined in Chapter 1, the degree of change in business and clinical outcomes, when compared to the total cost of the required investment, is the ultimate ROI and value measurement. While the healthcare industry has focused on implementing technologies such as EHRs with limited measurable results, the foundation has been laid for the journey to high-value healthcare. Transformation and innovation will become increasingly possible as the healthcare industry transitions from "keep the lights on" IT activities to focus on complex change initiatives needed to support population health management and the assumption of risks. Rigorous tools and methodologies are needed to support Rapid Value Assessment, Governance, Investment Management, Value Management Planning, Quantitative and Qualitative ROI and Value Measurement, and Value Score Cards. In the future, the healthcare industry must learn to change the way it changes through systematic and integrated business, clinical, and technology transformation.

Endnotes

1. Garets, C. M., D. Eastman, and D. E. Garets. *Change Management Strategies for an Effective EMR Implementation.* Chicago, IL: Healthcare Information and Management Systems Society, 2010.
2. Kotter, J. P. *Leading Change.* Boston: Harvard Business School Press, 1996.
3. "Change Management in EHR Implementation - A Primer." HealthIT.gov. June 2016. https://www.healthit.gov/sites/default/files/playbook/pdf/change-management-ehr-implemention.pdf.
4. International, Kotter. "How Have Kotter's Eight Steps for Change Changed?" *Forbes.* March 5, 2015. https://www.forbes.com/sites/johnkotter/2015/03/05/how-have-kotters-eight-steps-for-change-changed/#625fc8b13c7b.
5. Ashkenas, R. "We Still Don't Know the Difference Between Change and Transformation." *Harvard Business Review.* January 15, 2015. https://hbr.org/2015/01/we-still-dont-know-the-difference-between-change-and-transformation.
6. Anderson, D. and L. S. Ackerman-Anderson. *Beyond Change Management: Advanced Strategies for Today's Transformational Leaders.* San Francisco: Pfeiffer, 2010.
7. Kotter, J. P., E. Abrahamson, R. Kegan, L. Lahey, M. Beer, N. Nohria, R. Heifetz, and M. Linsky. "Leading Change: Why Transformation Efforts Fail." *Harvard Business Review.* August 25, 2015. https://hbr.org/2007/01/leading-change-why-transformation-efforts-fail.

Index

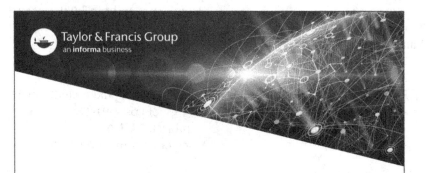